# HOUSESTEADS

# HOUSESTEADS

## A FORT AND GARRISON ON HADRIAN'S WALL

JAMES CROW

TEMPUS

First published 1995
This edition first published 2004

Tempus Publishing Ltd
The Mill, Brimscombe Port
Stroud, Gloucestershire GL5 2QG
www.tempus-publishing.com

British Library Cataloguing in Publication Data.
A catalogue record for this book is available from the British Library.

ISBN 0 7524 2890 X

Typesetting and origination by Tempus Publishing.
Printed and bound in Great Britain.

# CONTENTS

# ACKNOWLEDGEMENTS

ACKNOWLEDGEMENTS FOR THE FIRST EDITION

Near the exit of the Museum at Housesteads is a photograph of the Newcastle Training dig in 1981. It shows a group of largely smiling undergraduate diggers, the two directors Charles Daniels and John Gillam, and the present author. I owe a great deal to all who have worked with me at Housesteads and the Roman Wall over the past 18 years. Indeed it would be difficult to acknowledge all the ideas and inspiration that others have given to me. Of those students in 1981, I would wish to thank Derek Welsby and Alan Rushworth for the information used in the preparation of this book. And from that time also I am grateful to Stephen Johnson, the Inspector of Ancient Monuments for Hadrian's Wall, for the support he gave to a variety of Wall projects and for later commissioning this book.

In the preparation of this book I wish to thank my friends and colleagues at Newcastle University and in the National Trust for comments and suggestions, in particular to Lindsay Allason-Jones and Humphry Welfare for discussions about particular points. Rosemary Burton kindly commented on an earlier draft, Richard Bayliss helped with the final editing and my wife, Judy, ensured that the final text was a good deal more readable than I could have made it.

The photographs come mainly from two sources, the English Heritage Photographic Library and the Hadrian's Wall Archive in the Department of Archaeology and the Museum of Antiquities, University of Newcastle upon Tyne. I am grateful to both for their prompt assistance. Other sources are acknowledged in the captions. The location of an object is only noted when it is on public display. Almost all the line drawings and plans, except where stated, were drawn or redrawn by Alexandra Rowntree of the Department of Archaeology, Newcastle University, whom I especially thank for all the care she has shown.

At Housesteads one is always aware of the generations of antiquaries and scholars who have gone before. But I would prefer to dedicate this book to the present and the future; to my family – to Judy and to our children: Theodora, Tom, Michael, Freddie and Alexander, who have known Housesteads in all weathers for all their lives.

## ACKNOWLEDGEMENTS FOR THE SECOND EDITION

This book is a revised, second edition of *The English Heritage Book of Housesteads*, published in 1995. I am grateful to Peter Kemmis Betty for the invitation to present a new edition as part of Tempus' growing archaeology list. No new excavations have taken place at Housesteads since the first publication but since then I have been involved in a number of projects which have continued to examine aspects of the archaeology and history of Housesteads and the central sector of Hadrian's Wall. These have included *Hadrian's Wall, a landscape history* with Robert Woodside, (1999), an account of the National Trust's Hadrian's Wall estate, and *Housesteads Roman Fort Conservation Plan* with Peter McGowan and Alan Rushworth (2002) a very detailed assessment of all aspects of the site. I am especially grateful to Alan for continuing discussions and information in advance of the publication of the final excavation report due later this year.[1] This edition contains a number of revisions and corrections, some new text, especially in chapter ten and a new set of colour reconstructions of the fort and its internal buildings. In the first edition I made a number of suggestions about the fort and its history, some of which have been now confirmed by recent excavations elsewhere along the Wall. At Vindolanda, excavations in 1998 in the commandant's house revealed unexpected evidence of a late Roman church, almost identical in size and form with the building tentatively identified as such at Housesteads. Similarly at Birdoswald excavations south of the fort have identified a discreet area of settlement in the *vicus* associated with Housesteads Ware, a distinctive form of pottery connected with the presence of Frisian soldiers, a pattern first suggested by a reinterpretation of the finds from Housesteads.

I am grateful to colleagues at Newcastle University, English Heritage, especially the Photographic Library and the National Trust for continuing interest and support and for assistance with illustrations, particularly to Lindsay Allison-Jones, David Breeze, Hugh Dixon and Tony Wilmott, and especially to David Sherlock for his encouragement to use Philip Corke's excellent new reconstruction drawings originally intended as a graphics around the site – these alone can justify a new edition of this book. Finally I would like to thank Jonathan Shipley for assisting me in the preparation of the revised manuscript and illustrations.

# 1

# 'THE TADMOR OF BRITAIN'

Housesteads is nothing without the Romans. When antiquaries first saw the ruins of the fort at the beginning of the eighteenth century they were thrilled and astonished at what they saw. Political peace followed the accession of James I as king of England and Scotland in 1603, but it was nearly a century before the central sector of Hadrian's Wall was safe for outsiders. After 1702 the obvious interest in the remains of Housesteads led to a rapid succession of visitors and, their accounts over the next 30 years rapidly established the site's status as the most celebrated fort on the Roman Wall. To William Stukeley, who came in 1725, Housesteads was 'the Tadmor of Britain', a grandiose allusion to Palmyra, one of the greatest of Roman ruins, remote and then only recently discovered in the Syrian Desert *(1)*. Stukeley's description evoked not just the wealth of antiquities at Housesteads, but its isolation from the civilized world before the construction in 1751 of the Newcastle to Carlisle turnpike, normally known as the Military Road; an act Stukeley deplored because of the destruction it brought to the Roman antiquities. However the new road caused little damage to Housesteads and many could now take advantage of the turnpike.

> I retreated next morning over a moss to my favourite pursuit, which brought me to Housesteads, the grandest station in the whole line. In some stations the antiquary feeds upon shells, but here upon kernals. Here lies the ancient splendour in bold characters.

This description was by William Hutton, who will always remain the patron of Wall-walkers. He wrote of his visit in 1802, 'What can exceed the folly of that man, who, at seventy-eight, walked six hundred miles to see a shattered Wall!' Hutton's account, like many others, confirmed the primacy of Housesteads as the most celebrated and frequently described Roman fort in Britain. It remains so today, three centuries after it first became accessible to antiquaries, travellers and tourists. For Stukeley, Hutton and others throughout the eighteenth and nineteenth centuries, the appeal and fascination lay in 'the melancholy relics on the spot', and the crop of carved stones, inscriptions and sculptures scattered around

*A Cumulus of Roman Antiquitys at Housteads.*

*1* The earliest drawing of Housesteads by William Stukeley in 1725. Inside the fort, it shows a farmhouse built over the hospital. Note in particular the concentration of sculptures and inscriptions in the foreground on Chapel Hill and the slope to the east, what Stukeley calls 'A cumulus of Roman Antiquities.' *Robinson Library, University of Newcastle upon Tyne*

the fort and the surrounding fields. Most of these stones have now been collected in museums throughout Britain. Up till 1987, 60 stone-cut inscriptions were known, and the recent survey of sculpture from Hadrian's Wall lists a total of 132 stones ranging from figures of Gods to decorated window-heads and the fragment of a lion's paw. The early antiquaries were well versed in classical culture and saw Housesteads as a symbol of that world in a remote and devastated place *(2)*. In a modern age of 'sustainable tourism' and landscape studies, it is almost impossible to comprehend the horror felt for the landscape and setting of the fort experienced by these earlier visitors. Almost all the early accounts express this opinion to some measure, but William Hutton's observations on the way from Housesteads to Twice Brewed in 1801 can stand for all:

> A more dreary country than this in which I now am, can scarcely be conceived. I do not wonder it shocked Camden. The country itself would frighten him, without the [moss] troopers.

From Winshields, the highest point on the Wall, he wrote: 'The prospects are not grand, but extensive and rather awful.'[1] Attitudes to landscape and wilderness have fundamentally altered over the past two centuries, and the continued interest and popularity of Housesteads today can be attributed not just to the Roman antiquities, but to its setting of natural grandeur. Improvements in communications have helped to ensure the site's continuing popularity, but this did not come suddenly.

*2* Column drum lying in the fields south-east of the fort. One of two column drums in the meadow south of the fort, it is likely to have rolled down from the fort rather than being the remains of a distant monumental structure. *Author*

In 1911 there were 1,838 visitors, rising to an annual figure of 15,000 by 1939. The peak of 172,000 visitors came in the early 1970s before the Arab oil crisis discouraged leisure motoring. In 1996 the number had levelled off to 126,000 – nearly 150 times the estimated Roman garrison of the fort.

How do the two factors of archaeology and landscape combine to create a uniquely successful attraction on Hadrian's Wall? To the earlier antiquaries the appeal lay not just in the wealth of antiquities, but their setting in a near wilderness; the contrast increased the appeal of the ruins. Twenty-first-century visitors find the open, almost naked Northumberland landscape an attraction in itself and a relief from the claustrophobia of modern urban life. Yet there are a number of places of natural beauty closer to the centres of population where a similar landscape can be experienced. At Housesteads the archaeological remains of the fort and the Roman Wall are combined with the majestic sweep of the Great Whin Sill. It still feels like a frontier: to the south are farms and roads and the distant security of modern civilized life, to the north of the Wall is an emptiness, shadowed only by the plantations of the Kielder Forest. It seems, even now, endless without any hint of the Scottish Lowlands and the great Scottish cities of Edinburgh and Glasgow beyond.

This was the line that Hadrian chose as the fixed limit of his empire, and, standing on the north wall of Housesteads fort, it is difficult not to feel some emotion at the grandeur of the scene. The line of the Wall snakes purposefully to follow the horizon. It was a limit to the known world: within and to the south was the Roman empire, to the north was the territory of the barbarians: illiterate, uncultured and uncivilized, or so it seemed to the Roman conquerors (3). Unlike other parts of the empire there was little attempt to bring the subject peoples of the frontier zone towards a Roman way of life. Hadrian's Wall marks an extreme edge of permanent Roman culture in Britain. Almost nothing is known of the local native's response to the construction of Hadrian's Wall; if there was no direct opposition, there is certainly little evidence for collusion and there appears to have been a sullen resistance to the Roman military presence. Unlike southern Britain there is hardly any evidence for contact between the two sides and, if there was any change between them, it is not represented in the excavations of the farm-steads and settlements of the native peoples.

## BEFORE THE WALL

The creation of a Roman military zone across the Tyne-Solway corridor can be traced back to the governorship of Agricola (AD 79-85), in the reign of the emperor Domitian. Roman armies under Agricola pushed north of Carlisle into Scotland and in a series of campaigns, documented by his son-in-law Tacitus, the Romans conquered all of lowland Scotland and defeated the main Caledonian army at *Mons Graupius*, somewhere near Inverness. Throughout these advances garrisons were maintained on the communication routes to the principal legionary bases which remained at Chester and York. Two of the most important forts in the north of England were at the major river crossings at Carlisle and Corbridge. Initially these served as supply bases during the advance but they remained

*3* View of the north gate of Housesteads in 1909, looking east towards Sewingshields crags. *F.G. Simpson*

11

important to secure communications for the army in Scotland. Linking these bases was a road across the Tyne-Solway Isthmus, the narrowest route in England from sea to sea. This road is called the Stanegate, a medieval name meaning 'stone road'. The line of the road is known from the crossing of the North Tyne westwards to Cumbria and along it were a number of forts, including Nether Denton to the south-west of Birdoswald and Chesterholm (Vindolanda) to the south-west of Housesteads. In addition to these forts a number of watchtowers and small forts formed part of a system of surveillance along the Roman road.

The Roman occupation of Scotland ended abruptly, probably in AD 87 when troops were urgently required to hold back incursions on the upper Danube frontier of the Roman Empire (modern Austria). Many of the forts in Scotland were abandoned, including the partly built legionary fortress at Inchtuthill near to Perth. Tacitus wrote of these events that 'Britain was totally conquered and then let go'. Forts and garrisons were maintained along the Stanegate, but they only formed part of the Roman forces in the north of England and southern Scotland. There does not appear to have been a definite linear frontier in northern Britain at the end of the first century AD, unlike the formal boundaries which were appearing on parts of the contemporary frontiers in Germany.[2] The construction of a stone and turf wall by the emperor Hadrian from Wallsend on Tyne to Bowness on Solway was a remarkable and unique event in the history of Roman frontiers. Nowhere else on the borders of the empire was there such a short frontier line, certainly not until the building of the shorter Antonine Wall in Scotland. The decision to construct the Wall followed Hadrian's visit to Britain and its design must bear the mark of that energetic and idiosyncratic emperor. The scale of the Wall and its garrisons when they were completed implies that the Roman commanders perceived a real military threat to the security of the province. The only Roman source to record the purpose of the Wall, the life of Hadrian written in the fourth-century *Augustan History*, considered that the function of Wall was to divide the Romans from the Britons. Although this may reflect Roman preoccupations two centuries after the Wall was built, the statement remains a convincing explanation. Hadrian's Wall was constructed as a substantial barrier to the movement of the native, un-Romanised population in northern Britain across the isthmus. The building of the great ditch on the south side of the Wall, known as the *Vallum*, shows how this purpose was reinforced during the construction of the Wall. Evidence from the Vindolanda writing tablets dating to the very beginning of the second century talks of the *Brittunculi*, 'little Britons', a phrase which could either refer to Britons newly recruited in the Roman army, or to those who harried the occupying Romans on small light horses. The building of the Wall would have been a formidable barrier to such raiding, even if it were felt that this was a massive response to a minor threat.

The Roman army had proved itself to be the most efficient fighting machine in the ancient world against enemies who chose to attempt to match it on its own terms, but against less organised states without a formal army the outcome was less

*4* A relief of Victory found in 1852 in the roadway inside the east gate. A possible reconstruction of the decoration of the east gate is shown in *17*. *Chesters Museum*

certain. In these circumstances it is possible to understand Hadrian's Wall as a response to a continuingly hostile population throughout the north of Britain which could neither be subdued in a set battle nor cajoled into the luxuries of Roman life.

At the same time Hadrian was renowned as a builder of cities and monuments throughout the empire. He eschewed the military policies of his predecessor Trajan, but still needed military glory. This could be achieved in part by building a military monument such as the Wall, even if this might not count quite as high as the defeat of Rome's enemies or the conquest of a province; the construction of public works such as roads had been esteemed in Rome since the time of the Republic. Hadrian's Wall stood therefore as a symbol of the emperor's concern for the welfare of the provinces, but also as a symbol of Roman power and superior technology over her conquered subjects *(4)*.[3]

# 2

# THE BUILDERS AND BUILDING
# OF HOUSESTEADS

There are few archaeologists today who question that the Roman Wall in Northumberland and Cumbria was not started in the reign of the emperor Hadrian, but this has not always been so. In 1920, Professor R.C. Bosanquet, who excavated at Housesteads in 1898, reported one of the many Wall controversies he had witnessed as a young man in the following words:

> There raged with a bitterness which those of you who have the good fortune to be young can hardly imagine the controversy about the Turf Wall. When it was debated antiquaries used to bellow like bulls and good wives stopped their ears.

By the late 1940s however, a combination of the historical, epigraphic and structural evidence for the building of the Wall system showed conclusively that the great scheme was Hadrianic in origin and execution, and this view remains unchallenged. Excavations and the reinterpretation of earlier discoveries at Housesteads and on the curtain wall to the east and west have been crucial for the unravelling of this building sequence and there is nowhere else where the different stages are so clearly seen.

Construction work on Hadrian's Wall began in AD 122. It is probable that there were two 'building-teams', one beginning in the east at Newcastle, *Pons Aelius* (the bridge of Hadrian) and a second in the west from Carlisle and the Solway shore. In the east the Wall was built of stone, bonded with puddled clay, and was 3m (10ft) wide. This phase of construction is known as the Broad Wall phase. Every Roman mile there was a small fort or milecastle about 20m (66ft) square and between each of these were two towers or turrets, regularly spaced a third of a Roman mile apart. West of the River Irthing the barrier was first built of turf with stone turrets, and milecastles constructed of turf and timber. Later in Hadrian's reign the turf wall was rebuilt in stone. The frontier system continued beyond the western end of the Wall at Bowness, with the same sequence of towers and milecastles along the Cumbrian coast for a further 42km (26 miles), possibly as far as St Bees Head.

Construction in the east may have begun in Newcastle, although it has recently been argued that the builders began at the point north of Corbridge where the Roman road to Scotland (Dere Street) met the Wall.[1] To the east between Newcastle and the north Tyne crossing at Chesters, the Wall was mostly completed to this Broad gauge. Beyond the north Tyne and especially on the crags of the central sector where the line followed the Great Whin Sill *(colour plate 1)*, construction on the Wall resumed after the building of forts at Housesteads and Great Chesters at a narrower gauge of about 2.10m (7ft), known as the Narrow Wall and, it is this wall which linked the turrets, milecastles and forts. A further element was added to the frontier system with the excavation of the *Vallum*, a great ditch with high banks on the north and south sides running south of the Wall and forts. The *Vallum* can be shown to be later than the Wall and many of the forts because its course avoids the primary forts, whereas at Carrawbrugh to the east of Housesteads, the fort was constructed across the line of the great ditch, so was a later addition in Hadrian's reign.

The earliest Roman construction at Housesteads is turret 36B *(colour plate 4)*, the remains of which are displayed in a hollow midway between the north-west corner of the north granary and the north curtain *(5)*. Excavation in 1945 showed that the building of the fort itself was preceded by the laying out of the Broad Wall foundation and a turret at its correct location on the Whin Sill ridge a third of a Roman mile from its neighbour to the east. The Broad Wall was only constructed as a foundation, but the remains of the turret indicate that it was built at least up to the first floor which is consonant with elsewhere in the central sector where many of the turrets and milecastles were completed but the curtain wall remained unfinished in the first phase of construction.[2]

The turret is of a standard type, partly let into the south face of the Wall itself, with a doorway on the south side. A patch of reddened stone on the middle of the north side of the interior is presumed to be a hearth. This is the sole evidence to show that the turret was ever occupied, as no finds are reported from the excavation to help estimate the time span before it was demolished. Traces of the Broad Wall foundations about 3m (10ft) in width and surviving no more than two courses in height, were recovered during the excavation of barrack XIII and are also known to exist east and west of the fort. On the east side of the fort the Broad foundations have been recognised at the Knag Burn Gate and can still be seen in the broad culvert where the later wall crosses the burn. Like the north-west angle the later narrow wall butts up against the existing fort wall.

The sequence of building at Housesteads is quite clear: the earliest work was the turret (36B) and lengths of Broad foundation. Then work began on the construction of the fort and the north wall was set forward from the earlier Broad Wall line. It is probable that a ditch was dug on the west side of the fort at this time, but there is no trace of the wall ditch running down towards the Knag Burn. At some time after the fort wall was completed construction resumed on Hadrian's Wall, now built as a Narrow Wall to a width of slightly less than 2.5m (7-8ft) wide.

*5* Turret 36B and the north rampart looking towards the west. A third-century rampart building overlies part of the turret. The site of the late Roman church lies below the turf situated south of the interval tower and water tank which can be seen in the middle distance. *English Heritage*

What is not known is the length of time between the construction of the earliest elements, turrets, milecastles and broad foundations, and the later buildings, notably the forts. Most recent accounts of the building of Hadrian's Wall argue that the construction of the forts on the site of pre-existing turrets, as was found at Housesteads and Chesters, constitutes a radical change in the strategic organisation of the frontier, termed 'the fort decision'. Initially, according to this theory, the Roman commanders distinguished between the auxiliary garrisons held back in forts such as Vindolanda and Corbridge and linked by the Stanegate road, and the line of the frontier itself with its Wall, towers and small forts (milecastles) which allowed limited access through the mural barrier.[3]

There are a number of problems in understanding how this first phase could have functioned. It could have made sense in the central sector from Carvoran to Corbridge where the earlier garrisons were already stationed along the line of the Stanegate. But to the west these earlier garrisons were separated from the Wall by the rivers Irthing and Eden. To the west of Carlisle there is some evidence for earlier garrisons south of Burgh-by-Sands and Kirkbride, but the chronology remains insecure. East of Corbridge nothing is known of primary garrisons apart from a possible fort at Whickham and some evidence for an earlier fort at South Shields, but it is too far south and never formed part of the Wall system. The irony about this argument for a division between the garrisons and the Wall itself in this eastern sector, is that this is precisely where it is known that the stone wall was first built to a Broad gauge, whereas in the central sector only intermittent lengths of foundation was completed. How else can these changes in planning between the first stage of laying out the Wall line and the construction of the forts such as Housesteads be explained?

In the east the 'fort decision' is difficult to accept, simply because there is no evidence for the rear garrisons, whereas in the central sector the problem remains that the Wall itself was hardly started, let alone finished, before the construction of the forts began. The best evidence for this comes from Housesteads Milecastle (37) located only 400m from the west gate of the fort.[4] The earliest construction at the milecastle is seen at the massive north gate *(6)*. This was constructed first with a line of Broad foundation to the east and west. Looking at the inner face of the north wall it is possible to identify the two major building phases, firstly the gate piers and short lengths of curtain acting as buttresses, built at the Broad gauge, and then later the Narrow Wall. It is likely that the south gate built in a similar way is contemporary, but that only later were the north and side curtain walls of the milecastle completed.

Since the historical sources for the events of Hadrian's reign are very limited, to understand the progress of the building of the Wall and fort at Housesteads we

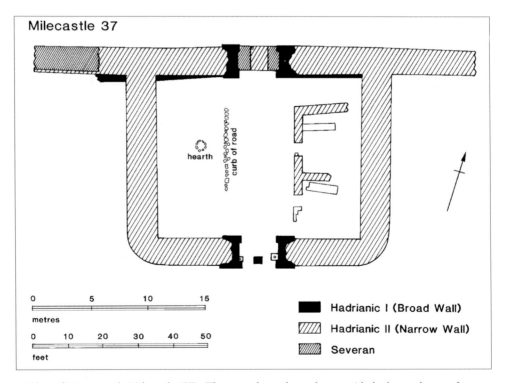

Milecastle 37

hearth

curb of road

0    5    10    15
metres

0   10   20   30   40   50
feet

■ Hadrianic I (Broad Wall)

▨ Hadrianic II (Narrow Wall)

▨ Severan

*6 Plan of Housesteads Milecastle (37). The stone barrack on the east side had a total area of approximately twice the size of one of the barrack rooms in the fort. This would suggest a maximum garrison of about 16 men outposted from the regiment at Housesteads* need to rely on the material remains as they have pieced together over the last century and a half to create a structural narrative. This evidence shows that before the fort was built on the crags at Housesteads, the Wall was simply a line of Broad foundations with a turret (36B) and at the site of the milecastle a pair of massive gateways — it is not known whether the tower above the gate was finished. The next stage in the narrative was the construction of the walls of the fort, but Hadrian's Wall, as a real barrier, remained incomplete until after the construction of the fort because at both the north-west and north-east angles, Simpson noted that the Narrow Wall abutted the curved angle of the fort wall: it was therefore structurally later, although by how much time we cannot be certain. A similar pattern emerges to the west. The next milecastle at Hotbank (38) showed evidence for massive gates and a north wall but little else at this phase, and this in a much more vulnerable passage through the line of the Whin Sill. The next two mile-castles, Castle Nick (39) and Winshields (40), appear not to have been built in the Broad Wall phase at all, although the foundation below the north gate at Castle Nick may indicate the decision to site a milecastle in the gap, associated with isolated length of Broad foundation. The same applies to some of the turrets in this sector, notably Peel Crags (39A) and Mucklebank (44B) (7). The evidence is inevitably incomplete, but more is known about the Wall in the central sector than elsewhere. Here the picture emerges of a continuing process of construction without the radical changes of policy which the 'fort-decision' theory requires, but with the inevitable human errors and mistakes associated with a large project.[5]

Hadrian's Wall was intended from the outset to be a powerful defensive structure with a strong garrison able to contain and respond to threats to its security. The construction of forts was neither an afterthought to remedy an oversight, nor a response to native resistance. The first phase of construction was to survey the line and begin work on the frontier itself. Once this was underway the site of the primary forts were selected and construction began taking priority over the completion to the building work on the Wall. One further element in the completion of the fully developed wall system was the construction of the *Vallum*. This great ditch located to the south of the forts and the Wall, quite clearly followed the building of the forts, as its line in many cases diverts to include them. At Housesteads, because of the hardness of the Whin Sill, its course lies further south on more tractable ground where a ditch can be dug, but the effect was to be the same. Once the *Vallum* ditch and banks were dug, access to the Wall, mile-castles and forts from the south was limited to elaborate crossing points opposite the south gates of the forts and nowhere else.

Although so many of the constructional details are understood there is still no clear indication how long this construction process took. Earlier studies have tended to create a rather tidy solution related to the surviving epigraphic record and the potential number of troops involved. There are too many uncertainties and variables to be sure about this and my personal view, based on a detailed study of the structure of the Wall, is that, although it was potentially feasible for the three

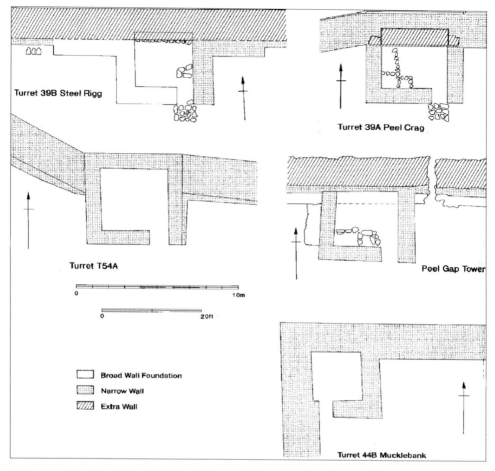

Turret 39B Steel Rigg

Turret 39A Peel Crag

Turret T54A

Peel Gap Tower

0              10m

0              20ft

☐ Broad Wall Foundation

▨ Narrow Wall

▨ Extra Wall

Turret 44B Mucklebank

7 Comparative plan of Broad Wall and Narrow Wall turrets from the central sector west of Housesteads

legions and their auxiliaries to complete within four or five years, in reality it probably took most of Hadrian's reign to accomplish.

## THE FORT

Relatively little detail is known about the primary construction of the fort since most archaeological investigation has been concerned with the later deposits lying closer to the modern surface. The line of the Broad foundations has already been mentioned immediately north of barrack XIII. Fragments of tent leather were found in waterlogged deposits below the east end of the barrack – evidence for the construction gangs living on the site while the curtain walls were being built. One other discovery reported by Collingwood Bruce from the nineteenth century was a cremation burial with a coin of Hadrian found in the north–west corner of the fort. This probably dates between the construction of the turret and wall foundations and the laying out of the fort itself, since the Romans buried their dead outside areas of settlement and would not have allowed such a burial once the fort was built.

The choice of Housesteads as the site for a fort requires some explanation. The system of milecastles and turrets is very regular along the Wall and such a precise system is rare amongst the linear frontiers of the Roman Empire. The location of forts along the line is rather more pragmatic and it is possible to discern some of the reasons for the selection of a particular site. Not all the forts on the Wall were constructed at the same time; some like Carrawburgh or Drumbrugh in Cumbria were clearly later additions. The initial scheme appears to have envisaged forts located about 13km (8 miles) apart, but there was clearly greater flexibility in the choice of site. At Housesteads a number of factors may be suggested, but underlying them all is a compromise between the military necessities of defence, provision and accessibility.

Housesteads lies to the west of a prominent gap in the Whin Sill escarpment, through which flows the Knag Burn. It is often said in discussing the site of Housesteads, that the fort commands this route through the Wall. Yet within a mile to the east and west there are other possible passages through the Whin Sill ridge, including Busy Gap with its medieval stock pound, and Rapishaw Gap where the Pennine Way leaves the line of the Crags towards Kirk Yetholm. Other factors must have influenced the choice of site.

The position is not ideal for a rectangular Roman camp and the west wall of the fort is vulnerable to assault from higher ground in that direction. It has been observed that a more level and broader site lies a little to the west, which had the further advantage of better all round defence. Three factors combined to determine the selection of the fort site. The first was water supply. As is well known, Roman forts needed good perennial water sources, both for the garrison but also for what was a requisite of Roman military life, bathing. At other forts such as Great Chesters, a simple clay–lined aqueduct ran several miles from north of the Wall to ensure a regular water supply. The central sector is remarkably dry, a fact which might surprise many visitors to a site with an annual rainfall of over 1.5m (60in). But wells are not easily dug through the impermeable Whin Sill and good water sources still remain a problem for many of the neighbouring farms. Other passages through the Crags are dry and the available water supply provided by the Knag Burn was probably the most important single factor affecting the choice of site.

Another aspect of Housesteads which again might well surprise many visitors is that it is relatively sheltered compared to other more exposed and higher points along the Crags. The land was renowned for its fertility because of the limestone which outcrops to the south of the fort. A colour air photograph of the Whin Sill will pick out the limestone–based soils by their richer and more verdant grass and it was remarked by John Clayton when he bought Housesteads Farm in 1838, that there was considerable competition and local interest because of the richness of the land. Similar factors will have encouraged settlement in the vicinity in the prehistoric and early modern periods of the site's history. Traces of early arable cultivation were recorded beneath barrack XIII during excavations in 1977 and further evidence for either pre-Roman or Roman Iron Age agriculture is known from air photographs to the north and south of the Wall and from excavations at Busy Gap, a mile and a half to the east of the fort.[6]

Most of the forts built in the eastern half of Hadrian's Wall were constructed so that the long axis of the fort was at right angles to the Wall and at least a third of its area and three of the gates projected beyond the Wall. This allowed easy access beyond the Wall and gave these forts what appears an aggressive posture. The best visible example of this is Chesters. On the Crags and beyond, most of the forts lie beside the Wall, and Housesteads, like the similarly sized large fort at the west end of the Wall, Bowness-on-Solway, has its long axis parallel to the Wall. Housesteads is amongst the largest forts (5 acres) and is unusual because the north wall of the fort was set forward of the existing Broad foundations and turret by up to 6.7m (22ft). The Broad Wall foundation occupied the true crest of the Whin Sill ridge but the fort was moved northwards to provide a wider, level platform for the granary with a raised terrace between the new fort wall and the ridge-top. At the north-east angle a fascinating detail of the construction sequence showed the almost inevitable confusions in a major building project. Construction began for a tower at the centre of the curve, like three other angles of the fort, but excavation in 1910 showed that work had started on the two side walls of the tower where they were bonded with the inside of the curtain. However, before the curtain wall had risen more than eight courses in height, it was realised that the tower would not overlook the line of Hadrian's Wall coming up from the valley, so the work was abandoned and a new tower was built a few metres to the north, allowing access onto the wall-walk on Hadrian's Wall from within the fort and providing better surveillance for the Wall.

QUARRIES

For the builders of both the fort and the Wall, Housesteads had a further advantage, which can still be seen looking south towards the Military Road and the car park. The scarp of sandstone on which the car park, Information Centre and road all stand is pockmarked with the traces of ancient quarries which turf and weathering have mellowed back into the landscape. Old quarries are always difficult to date without specific finds or inscriptions and it is possible that these could be connected with the construction of the Military Road in the eighteenth century. The central sector has plenty of stone but the right kind of sandstone is not always available and John Hodgson observed in 1822 that:

The stone used in the inside of the walls, and for other ordinary purposes, had been quarried out of the cliffs of the sandstone ridge, along which the present Military Road passes. The altars, columns, quoins and much of the ashlar work, have been taken from a stratum on the north side of the Wall, and similar to that in which the recesses, called the King and Queen's Caves, on the south of Broomlee Lough, are formed.

Hodgson's survey appears to be one of the very few attempts to study systematically the quarries in the Central Sector, typical of one of the most thorough Wall scholars of any age. He added in a footnote that an examination of all the rock faces near the Wall from Carvoran to Sewingshields revealed in one of these caves a crude outline of a figure cut in to the rock face, possibly representing a soldier, and a rough cross. The location of this carving is no longer known although it seems to be similar to a rock relief from near High Rochester in Redesdale, discovered in 1984. Since Hodgson's investigations, an inscription was noted in 1961 on the outcrops of Queen's Crags, recording the names of two centurion, *Saturninus* and *Rufinus*, and *Henoenus*, an *optio* or junior NCO, engaged in quarrying operations *(8)*.

The walls of the fort and many of the principal buildings used lime mortar to bond the building stones. This was produced by burning limestone in a kiln. The lime kilns which are to be seen today in the countryside around Housesteads are a tribute to the last two centuries of agricultural improvement and were used to make lime for neutralizing the acidic soils of the uplands. Despite the enormous quantities of lime that were used for the construction of the forts and Wall, only one Roman kiln is known from the whole length of the Wall. This was excavated at Housesteads by Simpson in 1909 on the west side of the Knag Burn, and fragments of pottery dumped in it indicate that it was used before the mid-third century *(9)*.

The kiln consisted of a circular chamber 3.10m (10ft) across, dug into the west side of the steep valley of the Knag Burn. Traces of a stoke hole were found on the south side and a long flue with splayed ends opened to the south. The shape of the structure is unlike eighteenth- and nineteenth-century kilns in the area which have pointed or segmental arches above the stoke holes and no flues. With its long flue aligned towards the south-east and from its location built into the side of the valley, the Roman kiln at Housesteads appears to have been built in order to regulate the draught caused by the prevailing south-westerly wind *(10)*. This is just the way described by Cato, a near-contemporary Roman literary source. The remains of the kiln were covered over after the excavation, but traces of reddened stones can still be found in the sheep scrapes at the lower side of the valley. No mention is made in the account of the excavations of the fuel used for firing the kiln, but among the layers of sandstone and shale there are often outcrops of coal which probably fuelled the kiln.[7]

On the north side of the Wall by the Knag Burn Gate, a large depression was known to Collingwood Bruce as the 'Amphitheatre', a place where he imagined

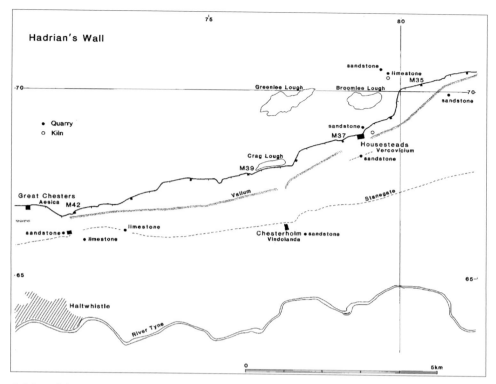

8 Map of the quarries and limekilns in the central sector of Hadrian's Wall

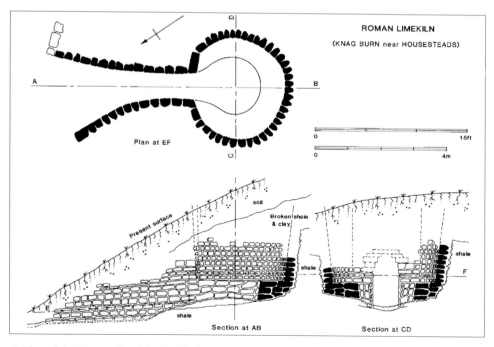

9 Plan of the Roman limekiln beside the Knag Burn. *After F.G. Simpson*

10 The limekiln by the Knag Burn during excavation in 1909. *F.G. Simpson*

gladiator combats for the entertainment of the garrison and where he noted that 'Nettles may usually be seen growing in bottom of it – a sure proof of human presence. Has the arena been soaked with human blood?'[8] With less drama, excavation by Bosanquet demonstrated that this was however another sandstone quarry probably associated with post-Hadrianic building work such as the construction of the Knag Burn Gate or repairs to the Wall itself *(11)*.

The site of Roman quarries at Queen's Crags has already been mentioned, but a little to the south-east and beside a limestone outcrop marked by lush green turf, is the outline of a kiln with a long flue of a similar plan to the excavated example from Housesteads. This is probably also of Roman date and the lime was used for the construction of the Wall on Sewingshields Crags to the south.

## COMMUNICATIONS

Before the construction of the Wall, the only formal stone-built road in the district was the Stanegate, running east from Vindolanda along a prominent ridge before dropping down towards Newbrough. With the construction of the fort a number of new roads were built linking it to the Stanegate, and the nearby fort at Vindolanda. Two early roads are known. The first ran directly south from the south gate and across the *Vallum* at a stone-built crossing. So long as the *Vallum* was maintained as a barrier, no other route could reach the fort and Wall from the south, except by one of the *Vallum* crossings. Another early road can be seen on air photographs approaching the east gate. It was later followed by the later Military Way, but it diverges off to the south-east heading for the Stanegate near Grindon. Both this road and the road heading off towards Vindolanda from the south gate must be later in date than the *Vallum*, but are probably earlier than the construction of the Military Way, which is thought to date to the later second century.

The course of the Military Way between Housesteads and Winshields is one of the best-preserved sections of Roman road in Britain. It runs between 50m to 250m south of the line of the Wall and today it is marked by a level green sward, especially clear under light snow or the parched turf of a dry summer. It is carefully engineered through narrow passes and across hillsides with boulder-built embankments. In places there were branch roads to milecastles, although no trace of one was found near milecastle 39 at Castle Nick. The hillsides on either side of the Military Way are pockmarked by small quarries used in its construction. Excavations next to Peel Cottage showed it to be originally 6.65m (21ft 10in) wide, with large kerb stones and a foundation of whin rubble. Later in the Roman period it was remade, but to a reduced width of 2.40m (7ft 10in), possibly indicating a change over from the use of wagons to pack animals for transport.

Despite the construction of the Military Way the Stanegate remained an important route and in the third century at least two, if not three, roads connected Housesteads to it. Vindolanda was unlike many of the first-century Stanegate forts which were abandoned with the construction of Hadrian's Wall and it remained

*11* The so-called 'amphitheatre' north-east of the Knag Burn gate, now identified as the remains of a Roman quarry. *Collingwood-Bruce 1884, 126*

as part of the frontier garrison up to the early fifth century. Indeed the fact that the two forts were spaced closer together than any other forts in northern Britain can be explained by the continuing importance of the Stanegate as a strategic route behind the Wall, and the access Vindolanda provided to the valleys of the South Tyne and the Allen. Further south stretched the Pennines, a hill country constrained by a network of Roman roads and forts stretching as far as York and Manchester.

North from Housesteads, the roadway leading down from the north gate was replaced by the Knag Burn Gate in the later second century. This was more convenient since it lay next to the bend in the Military Way at the crossing of the Burn. From there it was an easy climb to the east gate of the fort. The Knag Burn Gate seems to expect trouble, for it had two sets of gates at the front and the rear, not the usual one as found at fort and milecastle gates. No stone roads are known to have led north of it. Only three roads are known to have passed through the Wall: beyond Carlisle, from Birdoswald north to Bewcastle, and north of Corbridge on Dere Street to the forts in Redesdale and Newstead. From the Wall forts such as Housesteads, it is likely that any movement was purely military. In the sixteenth-century border wars, we hear of raiders from the west and north into Tynedale, but not of passage from south to north. Any long-distance movements in the Roman period, whether military or commercial, were likely to have been channelled on the military highways and not into, in Hodgson's words, 'the vast and almost pathless solitude of the forest of Lowes, enlivened with grassy, limestone gairs, edged about with beds of deep ling or impassible peat-bogs'.

# 3

# ANATOMY OF THE FORT
# GATES, DEFENCES AND RAMPARTS

The Roman empire in the time of Hadrian stretched from the Atlantic to the Red and Black Seas and around its perimeter were stationed auxiliary and legionary soldiers in purpose-built camps. The form of these forts and fortresses varied little across the broad span of the empire, so that the legionary fortresses at Inchtuthill in Perthshire, and at Satala in Cappadocia (now north-eastern Turkey) constructed within a few years of one another in the 80s AD, were similar in size and layout. The forts of Hadrian's Wall mark a turning point in the evolution of Roman military building. The reign of Trajan (AD 98-117) was a period of great military conquests in many parts of the empire. Advances were made across the lower Danube into Dacia (Romania) and further east to Greater Armenia and Mesopotamia (Turkey, Armenia and Iraq), but no attempt was made to return to Scotland, abandoned following a major crisis on the Danube in AD 87. Faced with troubles and opposition on his accession in AD 117, Hadrian followed a different policy from that of his predecessors and he chose to consolidate imperial gains in provinces such as Dacia, and elsewhere to abandon Trajan's conquests. He was later to claim, 'I have achieved more by peace than others by war'[1] *(12)*.

The Roman army was divided into legions and auxiliaries. The legions were highly trained (and better paid) regular troops who were recruited from Roman citizens and formed the core of campaign armies. Each legion was about 5,500 men strong, including many specialists, and it was the legions who were responsible for the construction of Hadrian's Wall. They were based in large fortresses at Caerleon, York and Chester, not on the frontier itself. The garrisons on the Wall were auxiliaries, raised from the subject peoples of the empire, most of whom were not Roman citizens on enlistment. A great incentive to recruitment was that soldiers acquired Roman citizenship for themselves and for their families if they survived to complete 25 years' service. The Wall garrison included both regiments of cavalry and infantry. A cavalry unit was called an *ala* (literally meaning a wing) and an infantry unit a *cohors* (unit or gathering). They varied in strength on paper from between 500 (*quingenaria*) and 1,000 (*milliaria*) strong. The regiment at Housesteads was normally a large infantry regiment of between 800-1,000 men. Infantry units of this size are unusual and the majority of the Wall garrisons were

*12* A keystone with relief sculpture of Atlas carrying the globe and flanked by two Victories. The sculpture may be interpreted as symbolising the world domination achieved by the Roman army with divine aid. There is also a pun by portraying Atlas on the load-bearing keystone. This stone is very weathered and for many years was built into the farmhouse at Crow Hall, near Bardon Mill. The families who lived in the house owned land at Housesteads from the sixteenth to the eighteenth centuries and the stone is likely to have been brought from a major building such as the headquarters. *Corbridge Museum; English Heritage*

mixed cohorts, *cohortes equitata*, composite units of infantry and cavalry. Cavalry regiments are less common and they were often stationed at strategic points along the Wall such as the river crossings of the north Tyne (Chesters) and the Eden (Stanwix). Large infantry regiments such as that Housesteads are also uncommon although it is less clear what specific tactical or strategic factors may have influence their location.

Auxiliary forts in the first three centuries ad were built to a similar plan familiar to soldiers throughout the empire. The outline of the fort was shaped like a playing card with gates in each of the four straight sides. Internally it contained administrative and official buildings as well as barracks and stores. The plan of an auxiliary fort derived from the temporary camps of Roman campaign armies, many of which can still be seen in the neighbourhood of Hadrian's Wall, probably occupied by the troops as the Wall was built. The fortifications of a stone fort such as Housesteads had developed from the defences of turf and timber forts; the rounded angles, internal towers, and narrow curtain walls backed by earth banks or ramparts were all derived from the prototypes of earlier, less permanent construction, when the army built such defences for their winter quarters. But as the tide of imperial conquest and expansion waned, so the auxiliary forts assumed an enduring form in stone, even if these defences lacked the sophistication of earlier, classical fortifications.[2]

The transition from the turf and timber forts of the age of conquest, like the early forts at Vindolanda, to the permanent stone forts of the Hadrianic age of consolidation, had begun in the decades before the building of Hadrian's Wall, but is nowhere so clearly expressed as on Hadrian's new mural barrier in northern Britain.

The plan of the external defences and the internal buildings was essentially the same in all the Hadrianic forts on the Wall (*13* and *colour plate 2*). The outline of the fort is frequently likened to a playing card, an oblong with rounded corners. Such a form makes some sense when building a turf or clay rampart since right angles in these materials are potentially vulnerable and the curved corner can be protected with an internal timber tower. The continuation of this plan in stone (or brick as is found in the eastern parts of the empire) makes little sense, especially as throughout their history of rebuilding and repair the interval and gate towers of the Wall forts remained internal, never taking advantage of projection to command more effectively the ground beyond the curtain walls. This failure did not come about through ignorance since the tradition of classical fortifications continued in the defences of Roman towns. It represents the triumph of a conservative military culture which ran parallel and distinct from the civic life of the empire – a military culture which despite some notable reverses, was continually victorious until the military disasters of the third century AD. Major changes in equipment, tactics and organisation only came about when the system established in the first century BC was challenged by barbarian invasions and earlier practices had to be abandoned.

The curtain walls of forts were narrow. At Housesteads it was only 1.30m (4ft 3in) wide, and on the outside it was topped by a parapet at least 30cm (1ft) wide, leaving a very narrow walk. In fact it is known from a variety of sources that these

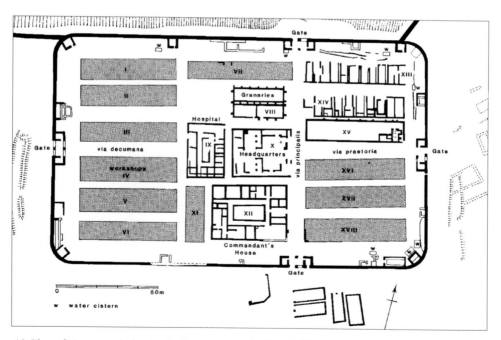

*13* Plan of Housesteads fort in the Roman period. *After RCHME*

narrow curtain walls were backed by either a turf or earth and clay rampart which sloped up from the interior of the fort. This allowed a broader walkway or fire platform as well as providing convenient access points on to the wall-top cut into the rear of the bank. The retaining walls for these rampart banks are visible at the north-east angle. Later in the history of the fort the rampart bank was removed and the narrow curtain-top alone sufficed for defence.

The curtain wall was built with roughly-shaped sandstone blocks bonded with lime mortar and similar to those used on Hadrian's Wall. These facing stones had a square face and a long tail projecting into the core of the wall. Each facing stone could be carried by one man so there was no need for complex lifting equipment. There was an offset foundation at the base of the wall normally one to two courses high. The foundations of the fort curtain and Hadrian's Wall are quite shallow and it is not surprising that in many places around the fort curtain there is clear evidence of extensive collapse and repairs. The core of the wall was of sandstone rubble bonded with lime mortar. Apart from the limekiln located in the valley of the Knag Burn, no other evidence for the use of lime mortar such as lime pits has been found. A feature of the primary fort construction, which can also be seen at north wall of milecastle 37 (Housesteads) and in an early phase of Hadrian's Wall at Sycamore Gap, is the presence of a course of thin flat sandstone slabs used as a levelling course at intervals of 1.2-1.5m (4-5ft) in the Wall face. This levelling course is to be seen in places in the consolidated north and west curtain of the fort and is probably the clearest indicator of Hadrianic work that survives.

The remains of stone stairs are found at the south-east angle of the fort *(14)*, to the west of the latrine and, they give important evidence for the height of the curtain wall. Four treads remain and if the line is projected they show that the wall-walk was at least 4.2m (14ft) above the outer ground surface. This is assumed to be the critical dimension since the ground slopes quite steeply to the south so that the inner face is somewhat higher. A similar estimate of approximately 4.5m (15ft) has been recently suggested from South Shields, based on the slope of the rampart bank. Ancient walls rarely survive to their full height, but evidence from the standing Roman fortress walls at York and from Worth in Germany where the full extent of a collapsed wall was uncovered, both confirm this estimate from Housesteads.

At the curved corners of the fort there were internal angle towers *(colour plates 3 and 5)*. These have narrow side and back walls similar to the thickness of the wall of a turret on the Wall. There were doorways at ground-floor level in the rear wall, although it may doubted whether there were internal stairs leading on to the wall-walk since the north-west and south-east examples have ovens on the ground floor dating from the first period of construction. At the north-east angle a drain was built in the tower to exit through the fort wall which probably functioned as a latrine. In the original plan of the fort there were only two interval towers built midway to the west of the gates on the north and south curtains. All the other interval towers were added in the fourth century when the defences were

*14* Stone steps beside the interval tower on the south curtain wall. By projecting the rise of these steps it can be estimated that the curtain wall stood 4.2m above the outer ground surface. *Author*

strengthened. The height of these towers is not known with any certainty – like the turrets on the Wall they may have risen one or two storeys above the wall-walk to a height of 10m (30ft). Fashions in the reconstruction of Roman forts and archaeological sites in general change from generation to generation, largely from a desire to be different, as much as from any new evidence. A current problem which has been much debated arose from the reconstruction of a full-size Roman gate at South Shields.[3] Among the issues that have been discussed has been the roofing of towers. Reconstructions in the 1950s and '60s showed a cultural difference between the supposed appearance of a Roman fort in Britain and in Germany. This revealed itself particularly in the way towers were roofed. The Germans invariably showed towers with gable ended or pyramidal roofs, a response in part at least to the snowy winters in south-western Germany. By contrast, in Britain, the towers of milecastles, turrets and around fort walls were frequently shown to be open and flat topped. There is archaeological evidence to support both these views. Stone roof slates survive from a number of forts and turrets, the cap stones from merlons of the crenallated parapet have been recognised at turrets and forts; but what is perhaps crucial and explains the recent shift in perception in

Britain from the open, flat-roofed tower reconstruction to the covered more Germanic style, is the contemporary failure of so many flat roofs constructed in the 1950s and '60s. British architects rediscovered the pitched roof in the 1980s and, at the same time recognised a key feature of the British climate – rainfall. Archaeologists listen to the advice of architects on matters such as stresses, loads and roofing, so not surprisingly, archaeological reconstruction follows recent architectural trends.

Part of the problem in understanding how the towers and turrets were roofed may arise because the structures themselves underwent major changes throughout the three centuries of the occupation of the fort and Hadrian's Wall. The merlon capstones already mentioned were flat stones with bevelled edges on three sides. They were placed on the projecting part of the crenellation to seal the top surface from water penetration. Roman illustrations of crenellations from mosaics show these capstones projecting so that the merlons are termed as T-shaped. This is how they are shown in *colour plate 4*. Capstones such as these have been found at turrets and milecastles on the Wall; they have never been found among the debris from the Wall itself. The evidence from the turrets and milecastles suggests that these were normally open-topped with a parapet. At forts and also possibly at milecastles, the parapet on the curtain wall is likely to have had merlons, and this could explain the capstones from Housesteads which are reused in the flagging of the east gate and in the floor of the bastle house by the south gate. The best evidence for the roofing of the gates derives from Hodgson's account of the west gate, which is discussed in more detail below, but which records sandstone slates from the floor of the gateway. He suggests that the gate passage was partly blocked before the roof fell in and was later covered by the total blocking of the gate. Whether these slates had slipped from the towers flanking the gate or from a roofed gallery over the gate itself cannot be ascertained. Finally in the controversy between open and roofed towers it is worth observing that on some surviving medieval towers there is a combination of a crenellated parapet with a shallow pitched roof over the tower which could satisfy all the evidence surviving from Hadrian's Wall.

GATES

Any fortification is a compromise between the desire to obstruct access and defend the interior, and the need to allow movement in and out of the defended area. Roman forts originated from the temporary winter quarters set up by the army on campaign and it should be recognized that these camps were not primarily defensive structures. Security and protection remained important for these garrisons but there were multiple gates allowing convenient access to the soldiers' quarters and offices inside and the easy mobilisation of the garrison outside the fort. Roman forts of the first and second centuries AD represent a system of fortification where the balance between security and access had tipped towards the latter. In the late empire after the crisis of the third century this balance was to be reversed towards defence.

A gate was critical in any system of fortification but it represented more than the necessities of defence. Gates were built to be seen. They were monumental because they could symbolise the military force and imperial power which the fort represented and contained. It was at the gate, the point of contact between the closed, Romanised world inside the fort and the open, potentially hostile landscape outside, where some of the principal images of imperial propaganda and display were placed.

Housesteads fort had four gates, one on each of the main walls; all are of similar form and the best preserved is the west gate. The main gate of the fort was the east gate (*porta praetoria*) from which a main street (*via praetoria*) led directly to the entrance of the headquarters (*principia*) (*colour plate 6*). Each of the gates had two arched entrances supported by stone piers to the front and rear. The arches and piers were built with large squared blocks, contrasting with the smaller, roughly dressed blocks of the curtain wall and towers. These smaller stones could be handled without the use of lifting equipment, but derricks and hoists were needed to lift the large blocks into position. Although these large blocks lack the fineness of ashlar, the blockwork masonry of piers and responds conveys robust strength reminiscent of the great stone built viaducts and tunnel entrances of Victorian railways.

The normal plan of fort gates on Hadrian's Wall was a double-arched gateway set back between flanking gate towers, with only the arches supported on blockwork masonry. At Housesteads the same double-arched gateways were used, but with a significant difference, since the gateway is only slightly recessed from the outer face of the curtain wall so that the quoins of the flanking towers continue the blockwork of the gate curtain. This has the effect of unifying the curtain wall with the gate façade and articulating the gateway as a bay in the line of the fort wall.

The double gates hung on turning posts not hinges, which were pivoted at the bottom in iron-shod sockets set in lead. At the top the gates turned in a projecting slab pierced with a hole, an example of such a slab lies in the grass just east of the Knag Burn Gateway and another was reused in the blocking of the north gate. When the gates needed to be moved it was necessary to cut a channel in the lower pivot block to allow the gate to lifted out and a replacement leaf inserted. Examples of this can be seen at the south and west gates. There was a raised doorstop in the centre of each passageway and a sill at the front. No gates hung in the rear arches. Each of the gateways was flanked by guard chambers with towers above[4] *(15)*.

*15* A reconstruction drawing of the east gate, based on excavated fragments of sculpture and decorative stonework. Above the twin arches there is a bold zigzag pattern on the architrave. This supported a dedication inscription which was probably flanked by two reliefs of Victory and Mars. An unusually large number of statues portraying these gods survive from Housesteads, including a figure of Victory found inside this gate (see also *5*). Above this was a gallery arched with single stone window heads, examples of which were found at three of the gates. The towers and the gallery are shown with tiled roofs, although a combination of open or covered roofs is equally possible. *Drawn by Kate Wilson*

## EAST GATE

Although essentially the same, each of the gates is preserved in a different way reflecting its individual history. At the east gate only part of the central pier survives. Hodgson records that when the gate was excavated in 1833,

> The main passage-way had been through its north side, as appeared by the worn state of its threshold and pivot holes of its doors, one of which formed a true hollow hemisphere, and was still covered with a shining blue coat of iron, from the friction of the pivot upon it.

The most interesting features of this gate are the blocking walls across the southern gateway since elsewhere on the fort these late blockings were removed by the nineteenth-century excavators. An additional room or shed was formed in the former passageway and when first excavated it was found to have been a store for coal, which Hodgson referred to as Crow Coal, a local name for coal won from outcrops nearby. His workmen lead a cartload away – what had once formed part of a monumental gate later served as the coal store for the fourth-century baths in building XV.

The wheel ruts and gate stop *(16)* in the north passage are well preserved and a number of re-used stone blocks formed part of the latest surface to survive. The gauge between the ruts is very similar to that adopted by George Stephenson for the Stockton to Darlington railway in 1837 and a 'Wall myth' developed that he took this gauge from the newly excavated east gate. There is a common link, but it is more prosaic and the 'coincidence' is explained by the fact that the dimension common to both was that of a cart axle pulled by two horses in harness (about 1.4m or 4ft 8in). This determined both the Roman gauge and Stephenson's,

*16* An engraving of the east gate showing ruts left by the action of wheels passing through the gateway. *Collingwood-Bruce 1884, 130*

which derived from the horse-drawn wagon ways of the south Northumberland and County Durham coalfields.

## SOUTH GATE

The south gate (*porta principalis dextra*) lay at the south end of the main road across the waist of the fort and led directly to the civil settlement. The remains on the east side were much altered by the later fortified farm or bastle house. Late Roman blocking walls on the east entrance were removed in the last century but the fronts of buildings B and C of the civil settlement project across the line of the approach to the east side, showing that it had already been closed when they were built in the early third century. It is generally accepted that there was an overprovision of gates in the Hadrianic forts on the Roman Wall. Many of those projecting north of the Wall were blocked off as redundant for the actual needs of the garrison and may be seen as architectural bombast. Where new gateways were constructed in the early third century at forts such as High Rochester, they only had a single passageway.

## WEST GATE

The west gate was called in Latin the *porta decumana*, meaning the gate of the tenth cohort who in a legionary camp occupied the rear, farthest from the enemy. At Housesteads the road inside the fort (*via decumana*) led to the rear of the head-quarters and was important as the principal vehicular access to the granaries. The gate is among the best preserved at any of the forts on Hadrian's Wall, rivalled only

*17* A sketch of the west gate at Housesteads, showing some of the blocking walls still in place. An account of Clayton's work at the west gate by Collingwood Bruce confused the arrangements by claiming that the one half of the gate was blocked on the outside and the other on the inside. This would have meant that the entrances were placed diagonally and 'forcible entrance by an enemy would thus be more difficult'. Despite Collingwood-Bruce's admiration for Roman ingenuity, this was a fanciful interpretation which can be corrected by the fuller account surviving in Hodgson's notebooks and this sketch from Bruce's own three volume copy of the Roman Wall.
*Hadrian's Wall Archive*

by the east gates at Birdoswald and Chesters. The two passageways are clearly visible, with massive masonry piers to the front and rear. The pivot blocks for both the gates survive in both passageways and it can be seen how the turning posts carrying the gates were covered to the outside by the projecting responds of the archway. On the south wall of the south passageway there is a square socket which is matched by an L-shaped slot cut in the central pier for a beam securing the two doors. A similar arrangement survives at milecastles 37 and 42.

On the outside corner of the south passageway, one of the stone footings projects in front of the responds and gate quoins. It is scored with setting out lines for the quoins, showing that it was originally intended to have a simple return at the gate like the single gateway at milecastle 37. Instead the arches and piers were recessed in an altogether more subtle gate façade, intended as a demonstration of military strength and recalling the triumphal arches of Rome and the major cities of the empire.

The reason that the west gate is so well preserved is that both the entrances were blocked during the Roman occupation of the fort so that the whole structure formed a solid platform resistant to later robbing. The course of the Military Way from the west was blocked by two banks and ditches which can be seen to the west of the gate. After Hodgson's investigations in 1833, the gateway was completely cleared by Clayton in 1850 and 1851 *(17* and *colour plate 7)* and a subsequent account of this work by Collingwood Bruce confused the arrangements by claiming that the one half of the gate was blocked on the outside and the other on the inside. This would have meant that the entrances were placed diagonally and 'forcible entrance by an enemy would thus be made more difficult'. Despite Collingwood Bruce's admiration for Roman ingenuity, this was a fanciful interpretation which can be corrected by the fuller account surviving in Hodgson's notebooks. His sketch plan shows that the north portal was blocked first with 'firm, strong masonry' and the south side was later closed by only a single course of roughly hammered stones 'with earth and large whinstones thrown behind it'. Below the blocking of the south gateway were found 'great numbers of nails of various lengths from 3–5 inches'. He continues: 'There were near the floor and with them broken pieces of slate and sandstone as if the roof had fallen in before the gate was walled up.' At Great Chesters fort, the next fort to the west, the blocking walls of both portals of the west gate remain in position and give a good idea of the appearance of the Housesteads gate before it was cleared.

NORTH GATE (*porta principalis sinistra*)

The north gate is similar in layout to the other gates and the squared blocks of the inner piers are well preserved (*colour plate 8*). The principal interest lies in the foundations of the gate revealed on the outer face, consisting of huge drafted blocks necessary to support the massive gate above. Originally a stone ramp of a 'solid mass of whinstones' led up to the west passageway, but this was cleared in the nineteenth century to display the massive foundations. Part of the roadway leading up to the gate was located in recent excavations 20m east of the gate and running parallel with the fort wall. It was abandoned by the late second century and covered in rubbish. The east portal of the gate appears never to have been used, but there is considerable wear on the west side and inside the fort deep cart ruts were found leading up to the gateway. It seems likely that the approach from the north-east became too steep as the road surfaces inside the fort were raised and the gateway was reduced to a postern. Nineteenth-century views of the gate show a narrow postern on the west side (*18*) and Hodgson reports that steps led from the gate down to a fine well under the Whin Sill Crags known as Mr Magnay's Bath. An alternative route from the north of the Wall was by the Knag Burn gate which allowed an easier ascent to the east gate along the Military Way.

THE RAMPARTS

In the original Hadrianic plan of the fort the inside of the fort wall was backed by a turf and clay rampart bank which was held in check on the inside by a retaining wall. This survived up to four courses high and was found on the north rampart to be 5.8m (19ft) from the inside of the curtain. On the east rampart south of the

*18 A detail from a watercolour by T.H. Richardson of the north gate showing the postern on the west side. Hadrian's Wall Archive*

north-east angle tower the rampart was 6.5m (21ft) wide, suggesting that the height of the rampart and hence of the fort wall, could have varied according to the ground level on the outside. The rampart constituted a transitional zone between the fort's defences and the garrison's daily requirements of food and hygiene. Apart from the gates and the interval and angle towers, the rampart bank was interrupted at intervals by bakehouses, cisterns and at the south-east angle latrines, all of which related to the daily life of the garrison housed in the barracks, but which were separated from them by the *intervallum* street around the interior of the rampart.

Bakehouses are found in the east and west ramparts of the fort as well as in the angle towers. The best example comes from the recent excavations of the north-east corner of the fort where the remains of the bakehouse survived under the later interval tower *(19)*. The building was constructed against the inside of the fort wall and was 3.4m long by 2.5m (11 x 8ft) wide, there was an entrance on the south side and inside were two ovens. The ovens had a raised stone flagged floor with a domed roof of sandstone rubble and clay. Reconstructions and examples of similar ovens still used in the eastern Mediterranean suggest that they were no more than 1.5m (5ft) in height. A number of Roman ovens are known from the *pistrinia* or commercial bakeries of Pompeii and these are invariably raised off the ground so that the stoke hole was at waist height, a feature shared by the oven in the kitchen of the Commandant's house at Housesteads and in contemporary pizza ovens. Yet many Roman military ovens known from forts in Britain and in Germany were normally entered at ground level and were not sheltered from the elements as at the Housesteads bakehouses.

Another early example of a bakehouse is recorded behind the east curtain north of the south-east angle tower – it was later covered when an additional watertank was built for the latrines. On the west wall the remains of a bakehouse with at least one oven survive to the north of the south-west angle tower. North of the west gate the two walls butting onto the west curtain wall show the position of another bakehouse with later additions planned by Bosanquet in 1898. A single oven was excavated inside the north-west angle tower and the upper course of the oven wall can be seen projecting through the modern gravel.

In the south-east quadrant of the fort there were three barracks and between the east gate and the south-east angle tower up to three ovens can be identified: two in the bakehouse and one in the south-east angle tower. Similarly at the north-east angle where there were two primary barracks the double bakehouse would have satisfied the breadmaking needs of two centuries. The pattern of surviving bake-houses is sufficient to suggest that there was initially a regular allocation of one oven per centurial barrack. The organisation of breadmaking by centuries can also be demonstrated by a number of quern stones marked by the name of a century found from forts and milecastles on Hadrian's Wall and elsewhere. A breadstamp with a centurial mark from Germany confirms this organisation.

*19* An oven in the bakehouse against the east wall, surviving within the fourth-century interval tower. *English Heritage*

The other main activity on the back of the rampart was concerned with water supply and hydraulics. Set into the base of the rampart and in line with the rampart retaining wall were a number of open cisterns. These were stone-lined and the joints between the slabs were caulked with lead and the bases sealed by waterproof mortar made with crushed brick (*opus signinum*). One such cistern can be seen behind the west tower of the north gate *(20)* of which it is recorded that one of John Clayton's labourers thought 'that the Romans used it for washing their Scotch prisoners in'. This tank abuts the rear side of the tower and it not difficult to imagine that rainwater was channelled from the roof or upper floor of the tower in to the cistern. The other tanks were partly set in the rampart, close to towers but not against them. At the cistern just west of the north-east angle tower, five segments of stone water channel were found leading to a notch in the cistern's edge and this gutter could have collected water off the metalled road surface. The proximity to the angle tower suggests some connection but how water was led into the cistern across the oven tucked in beside the tower remains unclear. From the known position of these cisterns the main sources were run off from the roads and the turfed rampart back. It is probably not coincidental that so many of the ovens and bakehouses have water tanks close by, since the main purpose of placing the ovens away from the largely wooden barracks in the rampart was to reduce the risk of accidental fire.

*20* Water tank behind the north gate seen in a view from around 1895, but now restored. *Hadrian's Wall Archive*

The two water tanks in the north-east corner held respectively 2,562 litres (563 gallons) and 2,340 litres (514 gallons) when full, probably sufficient for the needs of the two centuries quartered in the two barracks. Much of the time rainwater was collected from buildings and road surfaces, but in the driest spells water could be brought up from the Knag Burn.

LATRINES

Roman plumbing excites the popular imagination partly because of the special British fascination with, and horror of, the lavatorial habits of other nations, but also because it is seen as an element common to Roman and modern 'civilization'. It is not surprising therefore that for the majority of visitors the most memorable structure at Housesteads is the latrines, located in the south-east corner. There were other lavatories in the fort: the commandant's house and the hospital both have well-preserved examples of domestic conveniences, the drains from centurions' quarters of the barracks are thought to have led away from small internal lavatories, but the only other possible communal domestic latrine was at the north-east angle tower where the main drain under the *intervallum* street was led through the tower and out of the fort wall. There will also have been more distant latrines located in the bathhouse in the valley of the Knag Burn.

The latrines were built against the south curtain and the east and west walls butt against it *(21, 22* and *colour plate 9)*. They comprise a deep sewer flowing in an anti-clockwise direction around a central platform to an outflow beneath the fort wall immediately west of the angle tower. The central space was occupied by a raised flagged platform originally entered from the east end and the sewer pit was spanned by a continuous row of lavatory seats. The sockets for the corbels for these seats can be seen in the south face of the north wall of the latrine. None of the seats survives from Housesteads, but examples of stone or wood are known from other sites. Since no fragments of the more resilient stone seats survive, wooden seats are more likely. They will have taken the form of a continuous bench cut by keyhole-shaped slots. No provision was made for individual privacy and examples of public latrines from cities throughout the Roman empire show these communal benches often made of marble. The total area of the Housesteads latrine may appear rather small for a garrison of at least 800 men, but a similar-sized latrine is known from the legionary fortress at Caerleon in south Wales and this is thought to have served 12 centuries, or at least 150 more men than Housesteads.

The latrines were situated in this low corner of the fort so that surface water and drains could be channelled to cleanse the sewer and wash the waste into the outflow through the massive stone conduit in the fort wall. The system of drains still survives below the principal roads within the fort and the outflows can still be seen emptying into the top end of the sewer as a part of the flushing process *(23)*. The outflow sewer has only been traced a little way beyond the curved angle and

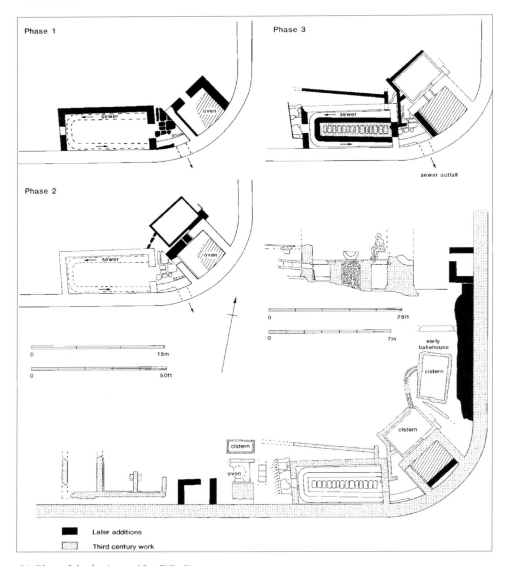

*21* Plan of the latrines. *After F.G. Simpson*

an attempt to locate the outfall by flushing coloured dyes through the system proved unsuccessful. A photograph taken in 1932 shows the stone lintel on the outside of the fort wall and a deep stone-lined drain with rebuilt fort wall above it. The east wall of the latrine is supported on monolithic lintels and a number of drains from the eastern part of the fort led into the top north–east corner where they are still visible from inside the sewer pit.

This system was only effective during or after rain. To alleviate this problem during dry spells, a large open cistern containing up to 23,800 litres (2,800 gallons)

*22 Right* The latrines from the west. *English Heritage*

*23 Below* The different periods of water channels at the east end of the latrines. *F.G. Simpson, 1911*

was built against the angle tower to collect water from the tower roof, at the same time blocking the doorway into the ground floor. The cistern was formed of carefully jointed sandstone slabs, one of which was re-used. The blocks were sealed with lead caulking – which survives in some joints – and held in place with metal ties. The scalloped wear on the slab tops, a feature of the smaller open cisterns, is more likely the result of washing the soldiers' clothes than sharpening swords or knives as has been suggested. Against the tower a thick layer of waterproof mortar can still be seen where it was laid to damp-proof the interior, which continued in use as a bakehouse. The new doorway to the angle tower was now opposite the latrine entrance.

When it was first constructed, a stone channel led from the base of the cistern to the north-east corner of the latrine and there is a notch in the top of the slab above the channel to allow the overflow to run into the latrines. A smaller cistern to the west of the latrines was set into the rampart back and appears to have been connected by a stone channel at the same time as the new south cistern was added behind the angle tower. Later an additional cistern was constructed to the north. This was of similar size to the south cistern and was constructed into the rampart bank at its south end and over a bakehouse with two ovens to the north. This cistern was lined with clay and only had slab sides to the south and west, a system of conduits led to the southern cistern. No trace can be seen of this water tank today.

During consolidation of the latrines in 1963 it was seen that the western end wall had collapsed probably at the same time as the fort wall and that a new entrance was constructed in the west, partly to reduce the weight at this point. The new fort wall was rebuilt on a slightly extended radius and the alignment of the first wall survives as a footing above the sewer outfall. Contemporary with, or a little before the addition of the north cistern, a new system of stone channels was provided around the south cistern which led water through the newly blocked east door and on to the water channel around the central platform. It can be traced in a clockwise direction so that the channel flowed the full length of the platform before emptying at the head of the sewer. On the platform are two stone water containers used when the water channel no longer worked. This water supply was obviously used for washing, although the conventional interpretation can be doubted.

Ancient writers such as Martial and Seneca refer to the use of sponges in lavatories and there has been considerable discussion and illustration in popular reconstructions of the use of sponges on sticks for this purpose, so the water channel at Housesteads is frequently called the 'sponge channel'. This however, raises a major problem since the 'bath sponge' is a Mediterranean sea creature and is not native to the seas around Britain. A feature of the supplies for the Roman army was trade over long distances: wine, olives and fish sauce were imported from the western Mediterranean, but it can be doubted if sponges were carried in large enough quantities to satisfy the lavatorial needs of the Roman army in Britain. A possible sponge fragment was identified from the Roman sewer at York but this is uncertain and it does not confirm the widespread use of sponges. What material was used as a substitute for this ancient lavatory paper is not clear. Recent excavations from the fort of Bearsden on the Antonine Wall suggest moss was used and there are a number of suitable plant-based degradable materials available in the area around Housesteads, including bracken. In Siberia snow suffices.

Most important, however, was the continued provision of water for washing and the water channel was an important element of the latrine. Midway along its south side the channel is so worn that water can hardly have flowed, showing why the central stone troughs were introduced. The exceptional wear at this point cannot be explained, but it demonstrates that this was the most popular place in the latrine as it was worn down by the hobnails on the soldier's sandals. Among the debris excavated from the sewer pit was a broken sculpture now at Chesters Museum showing a pair of feet with a sea monster and a dolphin. The figure was probably Neptune since these are marine creatures. Although only a small fragment survives it is not badly worn and it was finely carved. Another relief of Neptune, now in the Museum of Antiquities at Newcastle, is known from Housesteads. This shows Neptune reclining and holding a small dolphin and a trident while to the left are three nymphs. A circular hole cut almost centrally at the base of the relief indicates that it was part of a decorated fountain. It is said to have been found within the fort. The sculpture fragment from the latrine also formed part of a decorative water spout possibly placed at the east end of the latrine or else against the blocked entrance into the tower, to be viewed across the open cistern. The association of this sculpture with the military latrine is a reminder that it was part of a tradition of public hygiene and hydraulic display, also seen at the decorated fountain on the main street at Corbridge, and integral to urban life throughout the Roman Empire.

It has been suggested that there was an aqueduct leading to the fort from the west. Because of the hilltop situation this is the only direction from which water could flow; however there is no evidence either on the ground today or from past accounts that there was any adequate source in this direction or for a water channel. The frequent provision of stone lined cisterns in the Hadrianic fort indicates that water was either collected as rainwater or brought up in water skins from the Knag Burn or one of the Roman wells known from Chapel Hill or beside the Knag Burn. One of the scenes on Trajan's Column shows legionary soldiers collecting water in this manner and, at other forts such as Hodhill in southern England there is little question that water needed to be brought onto the site.

## THE BATHS

The Hadrianic bathhouse was built in the secure ground between the Wall and the *vallum*, sheltered in the narrow valley of the Knag Burn, nearly 200m east of the east gate. The baths were located on a level shoulder of ground on the east side of

*24* View of the valley of the Knag Burn looking south, with the site of the baths and the outline of the robber trenches in the foreground. The limekiln was situated on the opposite bank of the burn, seen in shadow. *Author*

the burn *(24)*. Little trace survives on the surface except for the lines of robber trenches following the stone walls, and a long cutting made by lead miners in the last century. Hodgson reports that when stone was being extracted from the site in 1779 the flues for a hypocaust were discovered full of soot and that an iron grating still survived in front of it. He considered that 'nearly all its walls to the foundation have been taken up, and the stones of them used in the field walls to the south-east of it'. Hodgson was overly pessimistic since a trench cut in the 1930s found one wall standing ten courses in height, almost as high as part of the baths from Chesters fort. In overall plan the baths appear to have comprised a long range of connecting rooms, similar to the plan known from Great Chesters and Carrawburgh.

The bathhouse was located in the valley of the Knag Burn to ensure a good water supply from the north. Bosanquet was informed that a line of stone channelling connected them to the stone-lined well lying east of the burn, but only the latter is visible. Nothing is known about the chronology of the baths except that in the fourth century a small bathhouse was built inside the fort at the east end of building XV. The re-use of tufa blocks found in the vaults of these baths could derive from the external bathhouse which had either decayed, or was no longer a secure situation, so distant and out of sight of the fort.

# 4

# ANATOMY OF THE FORT
# INTERNAL BUILDINGS

The interior of the fort was separated from the defences by the *intervallum* street or *via sagularis*, a name which translated from Latin means 'cloak street', but in fact has a more particular meaning as a place where troops could assemble. Within the fort the buildings were arranged in three blocks, centred on the intersection of the two main roads, the *via praetoria* and *via principalis*, in front of the principia or head-quarters. At Housesteads these roads led from the east gate (*via praetoria*) and between the north and south gates (*via principalis*). The central block of buildings west of the *via principalis* contained the principal administrative buildings of the fort, including the headquarters (*principia*) (X), commandant's house (*praetorium*) (XI) and the storehouse or granary (*horreum*) (VIII). In addition there is a long building (VII) north of the storehouse of which the function is not known. Part of this central range also includes two buildings set behind the *principia* and *praetorium*, a hospital (*valetudinarium*) (IX) and possible baths (XI) for the commandant. The rest of the interior of the fort was filled by two rows of barracks which were ordered to the east and west of the central range, parts of the fort called in Latin the *praetentura* (forward) and the *retentura* (rear).

The overall plan of the internal buildings at Housesteads was recovered in the summer of 1898 under the direction of R.C. Bosanquet and excavations over the next 80 years have revealed a full picture of the internal buildings of the fort.[1] Most of the central range buildings have been investigated in some detail, with the exceptions of buildings VII and XI. Of the barracks and other structures, only those three in the north-east quadrant (XIII, XIV, XV) have been fully excavated and are now displayed. The remainder (I-VI and XVI-XVII) are known only from trial trenching in 1898, but the outlines of these buildings can still be traced in the turf.

## HEADQUARTERS (*principia*) (X)

Early excavators of Roman forts frequently refer to this building as the forum, the public centre of a Roman town, combining the government, the administration and the official religious cults. This early usage, although incorrect, is a helpful reminder of how the plan originated and how the building functioned. In the temporary camps of Roman campaign armies, the central building was the *praetorium* or the general's tent which stood at the intersection of the *via principalis* and *via praetoria* and combined the role of command and residence for the general. In permanent forts however, these functions were separated so there were individual buildings for the commander and the headquarters, the latter combining the administration of the regiment with the worship and ceremonial of the imperial state religion.

The headquarters at Housesteads occupies a narrow platform and on the south side, although partly restored in 1898, there are fine monumental blocks used to buttress the downhill side and support an artificial platform of whin and sandstones *(25)*. Because of the difficulties which the site presented, the headquarters were considerably smaller in area than other comparable structures on the Wall. Wallsend serves as an example of a typical mixed infantry and cavalry fort of quingenary strength, that is about 500 men, and the total area of the headquarters is 720m² (7,750sq ft), by contrast the headquarters at Chesters, a cavalry fort, has an area of 987m² (10,625sq ft). Housesteads was built for a milliary cohort, a higher-status infantry regiment of about 800 men, yet because of the difficulties of the site the area of the headquarters is only 632m² (6,802sq ft), smaller even than Wallsend.

Headquarters buildings are usually divided into three parts, although at Housesteads, because of the poor preservation of the eastern end, this is not always easy to visualise. The main entrance was in line with the street leading from the main east gate (*via praetoria*), so that there was a direct view from the main east gate through the outer and inner gates to the entrance of the chapel of the standards. Another entrance led from the north side street into the cross-hall. The main entrance is marked by a single course of blocks and the shattered remains of the threshold. To the east of this a parallel row of long blocks probably marking a platform or the base for a colonnade later added to the east front. In the later nineteenth century, a sculptured relief of Mars was found between the entrance and the south-west corner of building XV. This was probably paired with a figure of Victory as decoration for the gateway and the same combination of military gods also adorned the façade above the east gate.

The first element of the headquarters inside the entrance was an open court with a colonnade around the south, east and north sides. Many of the moulded column bases of the first Hadrianic headquarters are still visible but none of the monolithic stone columns with a diameter of 0.40m (1ft 4in) now survive. When first built it would have appeared like a monastic cloister with the high wall of the *basilica* rising to the west. The west wall butts up against stone blocks at the angle of the court and it has been suggested that in its first phase there was an open space between the cross hall and the court. This is unlikely since there are no remains of pier bases to support this high wall and it would appear always to have been closed off. At the north-east corner of the courtyard are the remains of later stone flagging and gutters which survived robbing in the seventeenth century.

*25* The excavation and 'restoration' of the south wall of the headquarters building by Bosanquet in 1898. *Hadrian's Wall Archive*

A similar flag was discovered in the remains of the farmhouse at the east end of barrack VI. The gutter led towards the south-east corner where there was a drain pit possibly covered by a pierced drain cover; the outflow can still be seen at the south-east angle of the building. The later flagging in the courtyard is probably part of the Severan restoration of the building.

The west wall of the courtyard was probably blank, rising high above the roofs of the porticoes with a single doorway continuing the axis from the main gate through to the chapel of the standards. The doorway had out-turned responds, and a cornice block with curved brackets found near the doorway in 1898, probably formed part of a classical pediment (triangular gable) over the door. The pivot holes for substantial double doors can be seen in the worn sill. This doorway opened into a lofty cross-hall or *basilica*, lit by windows in the north and south end walls and by clerestory windows to the east and west. A row of column bases marks a massive colonnade to support the west clerestory and forms an aisle on the east side of the hall. The interior space with a high nave and side aisle was similar to a medieval parish church, the main difference being that the principal entrance was on the centre of the east side with the focus towards the west across the short axis of the building. Other headquarters such as Chesters have a matching door in the opposite end of cross-hall, but this was impractical at Housesteads because of the slope and change in level above the commandant's house.

*Basilicas* were commonly found in the forums of Roman towns and it is known from inscriptions that the cross-hall in a fort was given the same name. Like the urban basilica, its military counterpart at Housesteads was used as an assembly hall with a raised dais or tribunal at the north-west corner and a raised moulded base for statues or inscriptions at the south end. The remains of the tribunal survive today as a square mass of consolidated rubble, but originally this would have been faced with decorated slabs. The *basilica* was a place where orders were issued and the prefect could administer justice to the garrison and also to the surrounding district. Among the many decorated stones from Housesteads is part of a sundial, now in Chesters Museum. Sundials are known to have been set up in the courtyard of *principiae* to regulate the duty rosters, although here reliability must have been restricted by the constantly changing weather.

A row of five rooms led off the cross-hall to the west. The central room framed by an arch at least 5m (16ft) high, was the chapel of the standards (*aedes*), the place where the regimental standards were kept and venerated and the official shrine of the imperial cult *(26)*. Inside were kept the statues of the emperor and the imperial family together with altars to Jupiter and Imperial Discipline. One such altar is known from Corbridge, fallen from one of the *aedes* into the strongroom below. The standards were carried into battle but they were also venerated as religious objects and were decorated with flowers and paraded on religious festivals. Thus the shrine of the standards combined imperial ideology with military discipline and tradition in a sacred context. A recently interpreted inscription from the fort at Aalen in Germany calls the *aedes* the *capitolium*, the name of the great temple in Rome which was the shrine of the Roman state and formed the religious focus in the forums of many provincial cities. The *aedes* fulfilled the same role and stresses once more how the *principia* combined both the symbolic and functional elements of a Roman forum, in the same way the fort deliberately echoed the planning of a Roman town.

*26* View of the interior of the chapel of the standards during excavations in 1898; a voussoir can be seen resting on the threshold. *Hadrian's Wall Archive*

At the entrance to the *aedes* from the cross-hall is a heavily worn stone sill flanked on either side by shallow slots marking the position of decorated stone screens. The pier at the north end is cut to receive the stone screen. One stone from the arch was found in 1898, and a keystone with a relief of Atlas flanked by Victories probably surmounted it *(12, 26* and also cover illustration*)*. None of these screen slabs survive from Housesteads, but a screen from the headquarters at Vindolanda shows how the Housesteads *aedes* would have appeared. Socket holes are cut in the top of the slab to receive a metal grill and between these vertical bars the sandstone top has been worn in a series of scallops. This wear can be explained as the effect of the activities of the regimental paymaster handing over and receiving cash from the soldiers. Another more practical function of the *aedes* was that the standard bearer (*signifer*) was also the paymaster, responsible for the pay and savings of the soldiers. In many forts, such as Chesters and Vindolanda, an underground strongroom was dug below the shrine to act as a bank vault. The sanctity of the place will have ensured further protection. At Housesteads the Romans were defeated by the hardness of the Whin Sill and no strongroom could be dug; instead the north-west room was used, and direct access from the cross-hall was blocked by the solid platform of the tribunal and the room could only be entered from the adjoining room to the south.

The rear range of rooms on either side of the *aedes* are poorly preserved and have undergone many alterations, but they are normally interpreted as the offices for regimental administration. The recent excavations from the pre-Hadrianic forts at Vindolanda have revealed once again the quantities of 'paperwork' the Roman army could produce and it is worth recalling the example from Roman Syria where the administration of a third-century fort took over a neighbouring temple to store the papyri of the regimental archive.[2]

Below the *aedes* are the footings of an earlier wall. It is not clear what phase of the fort this belongs to, but it has been interpreted as indicating an earlier *principia* building. Recent excavations at the forts of Wallsend and South Shields have revealed that there were major changes in the alignments of headquarters while they are being built. This is likely to be the explanation at Housesteads, where the overall layout and most of the buildings appear to retain their Hadrianic position and basic plan.

The roof of the *aedes* is often shown rising high above the roofs on either side, but there is nothing which distinguishes the existing side walls to suggest extra weight at this point. The material of the roof is not known. Bosanquet records that numbers of stone slates were found in the collapse of the walls, but there are also many examples of ceramic tiles (*tegulae*) frequently reused. An explanation is that *tegulae* of traditional Roman form were manufactured locally for the building of the Wall forts and used in the main buildings at Housesteads in the second and third centuries. Later when these roofs came to be replaced, locally quarried stone slates were used instead on the buildings of the central range, the barracks and at the gates.

## COMMANDANT'S HOUSE (*praetorium*)

South of the *principia* and close to the south gate on a steep and terraced site is the commandant's house or *praetorium*. This was the largest single building in the fort and the courtyard plan echoed the pattern of town houses throughout the Roman empire *(27* and *colour plate 10)*. Originally designed to give shade from the Mediterranean sun, at Housesteads the inward-looking doors and windows gave protection from the prevailing winds. The officer in command, a *praefectus*, was a man of the equestrian rank, which gave him considerable social standing and his house reflects this position, particularly in comparison with the quarters of the centurions and the rank and file.

Because of the problems created by the slope, this was always a complex structure and, as with the hospital and headquarters, extensive stone-robbing has left a ruin difficult to unravel. The main entrance was from the steep *via principalis*, midway along the east wall, and the north side of the lobby and janitor's room survives to a considerable height. Originally the house comprised only the north range, west wing and a part of the east side. There is a clear break in the south wall showing two periods of construction. In the first phase the rectangle may have been completed in timber because of the difficulties of building on such a steep and damp spot. It was later finished using a different type of construction with long blocks laid as headers and stretchers. In the later phases these rooms were probably used as servants' quarters and stables with a drinking trough against the top north-west corner of the south-east room and another trough on the outside of the east wall. Both of these rooms have flagged floors and drains, strongly suggesting their use as stables. It is probably to these rooms which Collingwood Bruce referred, saying:

> At least two chambers in this part of the camp have been warmed by U-shaped flues running round three of their sides beneath the floor. These chambers when recently excavated were found to be filled with rubbish so highly charged with animal matter as painfully to affect the sensibilities of the labourers.

Traces of the U-shaped flues do not survive but anyone who has excavated water-logged deposits will testify to the malodour of antiquity which can remain in damp places.

The main door led to a vestibule, the place for a janitor and *lares* and *penates*, the household gods of a Roman house. To the right the modern wood steps show the problems of changing levels. These lead to a north portico, a covered walkway fronted by a low wall which supported the columns for the projecting roof. No columns have been found in situ in either this house or the hospital, but a number remain in the headquarters from earlier excavations, none fitting the column bases in that building and possibly derived from other porticoes such as this *(26)*. The rooms along the north side behind the portico and along the west side

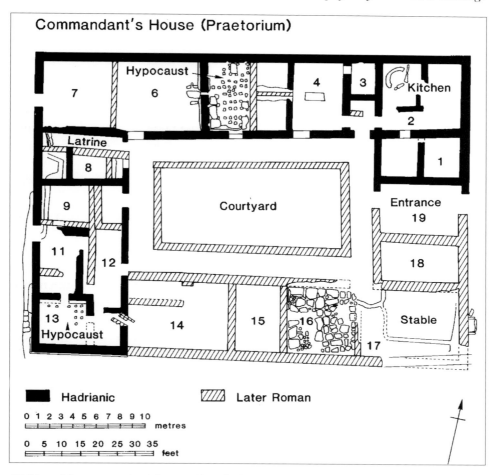

27 Plan of the commandant's house. *After Charlesworth*

formed the principal accommodation for the commandant's family. At the north-east corner is a kitchen described in 1858, when first excavated: 'it strongly resembled (though on a small scale) an Italian kitchen; there are marks of fire on its raised hearth'. In the north-west corner, remains of a raised oven preserved the re-used fragments of an inscription of early third century date recording the restoration of the *praetorium*. The other rooms in the north range underwent considerable alterations, reflecting the frequent changes of postings of the prefects who served here as little as three years. The small heated dining room is a late addition – it was suggested that this replaced an earlier bath, but this is unlikely and it was probably a larger dining room. There were other heated rooms which survive in the west range.

Between the north and west ranges is a corridor with a urinal and to the south a separate latrine with a stone-lined sewer, around three sides and a central flagged platform. The sewer ran below the next room to the south (9) and emptied towards the west. Finds from the sewer below room 9 included glass, samian pottery, five coins of late first- and second-century date and a gold signet ring, all pointing to the wealth, status and carelessness of the occupants of the house. Fragments of 13 blown glass vessels were identified, mostly bowls and beakers, as well as jars and a flagon. They are of interest because they represent the tableware used by a prefect and his family. The signet ring had a garnet intaglio engraved with the image of a theatrical mask. Pottery and coins suggest the latrine continued in use into the early third century, but the glass and ring are no later than the middle of the second century AD.[3]

It is unclear whether there were baths within this building but, immediately to the west, building XI has an entrance to the south-east and Bosenquet records an apsidal room at the south end which could be part of a bath suite. A small external cistern is visible at the south-east angle of the building.

## HOSPITAL (*valetudinarium*)

To the north and behind the headquarters is a building constructed around a central courtyard. The main entrance was to the west towards the *via decumana*. The northern half of the building survives very badly because, like the head-quarters, it was robbed to build a later farmhouse, shown on Stukeley's eigh-teenth-century sketch. The central courtyard was surrounded by a low wall supporting a colonnade. There was a long room on the north side, close to the main western entrance, and around the other three sides there were smaller rooms with a latrine in the lower south-west corner with a drain leading to the south. At this corner there is clear evidence for two building periods and the earlier south and west walls are quite visible overlaid by later cross walls. The latrine seems to have remained in use in both periods and the basic plan was unaltered (*28* and *colour plate 11*).

A tombstone from Housesteads records a doctor of centurian rank (*medicus ordinarius*) called Anicius Ingenius and doctors and hospitals can be demonstrated epigraphically and archaeologically from both legionary fortresses and auxiliary forts. This building at Housesteads was probably a hospital and an identical structure at Wallsend is of the same size and plan, although neither of these buildings have produced independent evidence to confirm the identification. An alternative might be an armoury or workshops but these can be more positively identified with buildings IV and XV at Housesteads. The presence of latrines and carefully laid out rooms makes a hospital a most likely interpretation. It also shows the concern felt by the emperors for the welfare of the army, a concern not shown to ordinary citizens. Although in an age before antiseptics, as in early nineteenth-century lying-in hospitals, this might have been a mixed blessing for the sick and wounded.

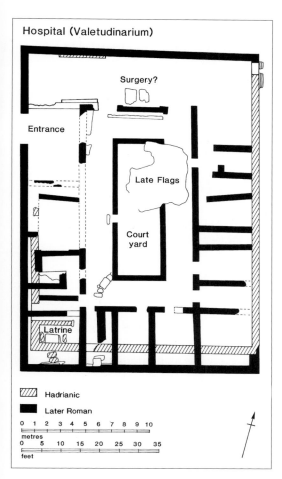

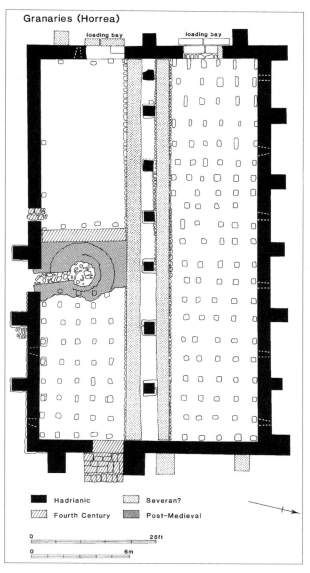

*28 Above* Plan of the hospital.
*After Charlesworth*

*29 Right* Plan of the granaries

## GRANARIES (*horrea*)

The granaries are built on the highest part of the fort astride the level crest of the Whin Sill escarpment. The need to secure a level, dry spot for the granaries determined the move of the north curtain beyond the line of the Broad foundations and the site of turret 36B. Since the eighteenth century the granaries have been noted as the most prominent building in the fort and Horsley identified their conspicuous mound as the *praetorium* by which he meant the headquarters building. The earliest accurate survey of Housesteads and its landscape in 1852 shows the granaries as the only visible building inside the fort.

All Roman forts had granaries so that sufficient foodstuffs could be kept in reserve for campaign or siege. The main commodity was grain, most probably stored in sacks against the walls; burnt grain has been discovered in the granaries at South Shields, but other foodstuffs including meat could be kept in this cool and dry place. The external walls are very substantial and they are buttressed on the exterior. It is not known if there was an upper storey, but the walls are solid enough to have supported one.

The original Hadrianic granary was a wide single hall measuring internally 23.75m long and 13m wide (78 x 43ft), and divided by a row of six stone piers, with moulded bases and capitals which remain between the later dividing walls *(29 and colour plate 12)*. These large piers up to 0.63sqm (7sq ft) supported a double span roof across the two aisles of the granary. There were two entrances at the west end, originally 2.40m (8ft) wide, and the north doorway has a finely preserved door check and pivot plates cut into the threshold blocks. Goods access to the fort at this period was from the west gate and there was an open area to the west of the granary for carts to unload and turn. This route from the west reduced congestion and noise on the main street from the east gate, which was the only alternative approach because of the steep slope to the south. There was a broad roof with a wide eaves-drip supported by the buttresses, to ensure that the base of the walls remained dry. Support of this roof overhang was probably the main function of the buttresses since the lateral pressure from the grain inside was probably not as great as has been estimated.

A common feature in most military granaries was a raised floor which ensured that the foodstuffs were kept dry and might help the control of vermin. Around the outer wall were vents to ensure the circulation of air below the floor and on the south wall two of the vents have a shallow setting for two mullions similar to those which are still in place at Corbridge. The vents are a feature of the primary granary, but the stone pillars belong to the subsequent phase, so that it is unknown how the raised floor was supported in the first phase. An alternative to pillars was the use of dwarf walls to be seen at Corbridge and Birdoswald, but there is no evidence for these until the fourth century at Housesteads.

This two-aisled granary was altered by the addition of first one and then a second cross-wall from east to west. The central piers were dismantled and many of the capitals survive resting on the bases. The footings of the south dividing wall partly include these bases, and suggesting that this wall was built while the piers were still standing; indeed they could have been incorporated to act as buttresses for a reduced south granary standing alone. Built in the south dividing wall, on the north face at the east end was a small inscription: COH I TV *(cohors I Tungrorum)*. It is set upside down and so was apparently re-used after the Tungrians had already served in the garrison. It is likely that the second cross-wall was added soon after the southern one since both granaries have identical flooring with main joists supported on rough stone pillars with square sockets and a ledge in both of the later dividing walls. The joists rested against the earlier external walls *(30)*.

*30* Reconstruction drawing of the north granary. *After Rena Gardiner*

One of the frustrations of studying the granaries is the realisation that they were largely unexcavated until 1930 when the site was given to the National Trust, when they were cleared with virtually no archaeological record. The structural evidence from the cross-walls suggests that there was a phase when less than half the granary storage was required, and even when the two granaries were built the total floor space was reduced by 18%. Once the two new granaries were built there were separate ridged roofs with a gully above the earlier piers. The implications of these alterations are difficult to assess. But if the changes in the storage area in the granaries reflect the size of the garrison and any dependent units in milecastles, the south granary may have been built during or immediately following the advance of the garrisons on to the Antonine Wall, either for a caretaker garrison or after a partial withdrawal. Similarly the provision of a second granary may represent the garrison brought back to full strength some time later in the second century. The subsequent history of the granaries is considered in a later chapter.

Bosanquet's excavations recovered the outline plan of a building (VII) to the north of the granaries. This is similar in dimensions to a barrack, but the only remains to be seen of it over the south side of turret 36B show features similar to the later barrack units or chalets, with little evidence for an earlier second-century structure below.

## BARRACKS

The east and west blocks of the fort each contain six buildings, ten of which were barracks from the earliest phase *(colour plate 5)*. All these buildings were aligned east to west, so they could be terraced across the hillside and faced either south or north. It is common in many forts for barracks to be arranged in pairs across a roadway or back-to-back. Because of the steep ground this could not always be achieved, so that only barracks II and III face one another, but all the others do not, even where there is a street between them.

Only barracks XIII and XIV and building XV have been fully excavated in recent times *(colour plate 13)* and the remainder are only known from Bosanquet's trenches. Barracks XIII and XIV show that the early barracks had a veranda and a gutter facing onto the street and this pattern can be recognized from the 1898 plan despite the later alterations which are also shown. On the basis of this it is possible to show that the earliest fort had ten barracks. The standard form of the early barracks was a long building, subdivided into ten units (*contubernia*), with separate larger apartments for the centurion at the end facing the *intervallum* street where he would have lived with household slaves and possibly his family. Along the length of the building in front of the barrack rooms was a veranda and, a gutter marks the position of the eaves-drip above. The veranda was supported on timber or stone piers with moulded stone bases. The centurion's quarters projected beyond the line of the barrack rooms up to the veranda, so that in plan the barracks had a shallow L-shape *(54)*. Unlike the central buildings which were stone-built throughout, the barracks were half-timbered, with low walls of sandstone rubble bonded with clay supporting timber uprights and frame, filled with wattle and daub. The roofs of many of the barracks ran simply with a single ridge from west to east, but in the east part of the fort, because the ground slopes down to the east, the roofline must have stepped down like the terraced roofs of a northern milltown.

The number of men in a century remains a problem for students of the Roman army. Century (*centuria*) was used in Latin as a notional figure of quantity, as well as an exact one. Thus the English names for centipedes and millipedes derive from the Latin names for these insects and, are meant to convey large and larger numbers of feet, not precise figures. Similarly the use of *centuria* in different Roman sources need not be consistent or precise. At the time of Hadrian a century could mean between 80 to 100 men, although the lower figure seems to be more commonly used. At Housesteads there are ten *contubernia* in each barrack, so that if each unit held a maximum of eight men, it implies a total strength of 80 men. This represents the potential size of century envisaged when the barracks were built, but we cannot expect that number of men to have been consistently maintained over any length of time. These units were subdivided into a front room (*arma*) for storing equipment and a rear room (*papilio*) for sleeping. In *contubernium* 3 (numbered from the east) in barrack XIII the north room (*arma*) was 2.15m by 3.6m (7 x 12ft) and the south room (*papilio*) was rather larger 4.65m by 3.6m (15

*31 A relief of Victory standing on a globe. Stukeley saw it 'lying in the meadow fronting the station' in 1725. The figure derives from a Hellenistic form which can be traced back to the fifth century BC*

x 12ft). There is no evidence for bunk beds, sometimes suggested in reconstructions of *contubernia*, and the soldiers probably slept on palliasses with sufficient room for eight men. Some forts, such as Wallsend, have shown that there was a window in the rear wall, because a dump of pottery in the alley between two back-to-back barracks could only have been thrown from a rear window.

The centurion's quarters and *contubernia* of barrack XIII remained without major alterations until the later third century when they were rebuilt as 'chalets'. There were a number of internal additions to the centurion's quarters, new floors were laid and hearths. Similarly in the barrack, although few of the rooms were fully investigated, in some there were up to six changes in floors with new hearths and traces of charcoal where braziers had stood. There appeared to be few other significant alterations over a century and a half, let alone evidence for abandonment of the fort during the occupation of the Antonine Wall as might be expected. The floors were sometimes flagged, but the relative cleanliness overall suggests there were wooden floors which were kept clean, but have left no trace. This is quite unlike the interior of milecastle 39 at the same period which has rougher internal building with much less overall concern for tidiness.

In both the *praetentura* (east range) and *retentura* (west range), five of the six buildings can be interpreted as barracks, but two buildings, IV and XV, seem in all periods to have had a different use. Both front on to two of the main streets in the fort. Building IV was investigated by Bosanquet, who described it as the 'Iron works' based on the discovery of iron slag and burnt clay. The walls were deeply buried compared with other buildings and he supposed that it had collapsed and had not been rebuilt. Traces of later chalet type barracks were not found. Another unusual feature was 'considerable bodies of clay' which extended across the street to the barrack opposite. Such a quantity of clay has not been seen elsewhere at Housesteads, but could represent the collapse of a mud-brick wall built on stone footings. This would be a more fire resistant material if smelting and metalworking were carried out. Although this might appear to be a rather exotic building material for Northumberland, mud-brick construction or 'dubbins' is part of the vernacular building tradition in the Cumbrian villages on the south side of the Solway.

## BUILDING XV

Building XV faces on to the *via praetoria* and the visible structure dates from the fourth century. Below this the remains of three buildings have been found, all similar in length to a barrack block, but of varying widths. The total width of barracks XIII and XIV is 11m (36ft) from the veranda gutter to the outer face of the back wall. This is the same dimension as the massive stone phase of the latest building XV, but the earlier structures had a maximum width of only 9.5m (31ft). The remains of these early structures were only found at the east end, disturbed by the later baths. It is difficult to interpret either of these early phases as a conventional barrack, partly because of its narrowness and also because there is no evidence for the wider centurion's quarters at the east end. Phase one was possibly a storebuilding or armoury conveniently situated beside a principal street. There is evidence for an armourer (*custos armorum*) from an inscribed altar to Mars and Victory, which has been found at the fort. Later in the fourth century an armoury is known from the north-east room in the headquarters. The next phase in building XV was perhaps a barrack with a veranda pier, and cross walls and evidence of domestic hearths. The third, and final phase before it was rebuilt as a massive stone building, saw the construction of an open hall 9m (30ft) wide with two stone-flagged drains running towards the east; no trace of this phase was found at the west end since all the early deposits were removed by the later builders. The third phase with large drains appears to have been stables, once more reverting from domestic to service use, in a convenient place close to the centre of the fort and the main gate.

# 5

# VERCOVICIUM: THE ANCIENT NAME AND GARRISONS

An early fifth-century document, the *Notitia Dignitatum*, lists *Borcovicus* among the forts on Hadrian's Wall and this form often occurs in modern accounts as the ancient name for Housesteads. An altar from Housesteads dedicated to Mars, however, gives a regiment of Frisians the abbreviated epithet *VER*, showing the initial letters of the place name, which can be expanded as *Vercovicium*. This has been interpreted to mean 'hilly place' in Celtic, as if that was the local name which the Romans adopted. A more recent study of the place names in Roman Britain has observed that among the forts and other military posts, Latin names are very rare and that normally native Celtic names were adopted and, in some cases coined. The preferred translation of *Vercovicium* is 'place of the effective fighters', the name applied by Celtic speakers to the first Roman garrison of the fort. Whether this was a perspective favoured by the natives or an official creation is not known.[1]

The original Hadrianic fort had at least ten barracks, sufficient for a *cohors milliaria*, an infantry regiment of about 800 men *(32)*. The earliest garrison is not known with certainty, but *cohors I Tungrorum milliaria*, 'the first cohort of Tungrians a thousand strong', is recorded on inscriptions from the site by about AD 200. *Tungria* was a district in the province of *Gallia Belgica*, today the region of Tongres and Maastricht in southern Belgium and Holland. The Tungrians were a Germanic tribe who had crossed the Rhine in the first century BC and the earliest known regiments were raised in Gaul and formed part of Vitellius' defeated army in southern Gaul during the civil wars of AD 69. By AD 83, two cohorts of Tungrians were serving in Britain with Agricola's army in Scotland, and fought at the battle of *Mons Graupius*. After the withdrawal of Roman armies from Scotland in Trajan's reign, the First cohort of Tungrians is recorded among the regiments stationed at Vindolanda.

The recent discoveries of writing tablets and other objects at Vindolanda make the First Tungrians among the best-known units in the Roman army. A strength report found in 1988 and dated from its archaeological context to around AD 90, gives the total number of men in *cohors I Tungrorum*, under the command of the prefect *Iulius Verecundus*, as 752, of which only one centurion and 296 men were

*32* A collection of inscribed fragments from Housesteads, now in the Chesters Museum.
*Hadrian's Wall Archive*

present at the fort. Of the remainder, 336 men and two centurions were at *Coria* (Corbridge), 46 were serving on the provincial governor's staff, 1 centurion was on special detachment in London and the remaining 45 men were in four separate, but unidentified postings. From those in garrison, 31 men (more than 10%) were unfit for duty, 15 were ill, 6 were wounded and 10 had eye infections, probably conjunctivitis or general inflammations. The fort's hospital mentioned in the writing tablets was clearly kept busy.[2]

The regiment as recorded on this report was clearly of milliary strength by this time, even if this fact does not appear on its title. The dispersal of soldiers, not only on attachment to the provincial governor, but in detachments elsewhere in the frontier zone might surprise those who view the Roman army as a system of model regularity. But this document illustrates how the actual size and organization of auxiliary units were liable to local variation. Between AD 90 and AD 120, evidence from the writing tablets at Vindolanda *(33)* suggests that as well as the Tungrians, the fort was occupied by at least two auxiliary cohorts of Batavians, detachments of legionary soldiers and *equites Vardulli*. Some of these units must have formed combined garrisons.

In AD 103 the First Tungrians are first attested as being of milliary strength, but contrary to the general rule and, like their sister regiment the Second Milliary Cohort of Tungrians, part mounted with Latin rights, which served at Birrens and Castlesteads, on Hadrian's Wall, the commanding officer unusually had the rank of *praefectus*, rather than that of tribune. The discovery at Vindolanda of a diploma, a pair of bronze tablets recording soldiers' privileges and often granting

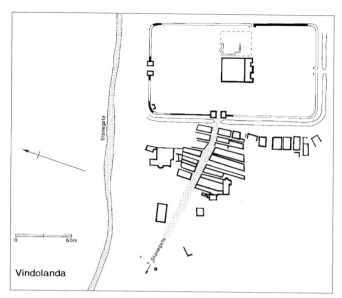

33 Comparative plans of the stone forts and civil settlements at Vindolanda (*right*) and Housesteads (*below*). The important finds of writing tablets at Vindolanda come from earlier timber forts, not visible on this plan

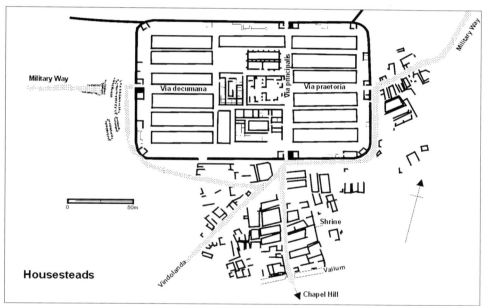

citizenship for themselves and their children, issued in AD 146 to a soldier of the First Tungrians, suggests that he may have served there when first recruited in AD 121 and later returned for retirement. Further evidence comes from a spearhead with the punched inscription TUNG, from a floor dating from the 120s or later. Both pieces of evidence suggest the unit was in garrison at the time of the construction of Hadrian's Wall and possibly throughout Hadrian's reign. It seems that the veteran returned to his place of enlistment to retire, since by AD 146 the cohort was in garrison at Castlecary on the Antonine Wall (RIB 2156). A tombstone discovered at Vindolanda in 1997 commemorates a legionary centurion in command of the First Tungrians who was killed in battle (*in bello…interfectus*). The date is not given but a number of scholars have suggested that he may have died fighting the British tribes during Hadrian's reign.[3] Apart from the evidence from Vindolanda, a building inscription from Carrawburgh (Wright 1966, 218, 5) indicates their involvement in construction work on the fort, although from the same period there is also another inscription recording work by the First cohort of Aquitanians (RIB 1550). But neither regiment was necessarily in garrison, similarly a stamped brick of the First Tungrians from Hare Hill, west of the fort at Birdoswald (RIB 2477), does not demonstrate that they were garrisoned at Birdoswald in the Hadrianic period, although that forts like Housesteads were clearly laid out with the intention of housing a large double-strength milliary unit.

From Housesteads there is no epigraphic evidence for an early garrison and it is normally assumed that the earliest positive evidence for the Tungrians does not date before *c.*AD 200. The size of the fort and its internal arrangements with at least ten barracks implies that from the outset it was intended for a milliary cohort and, it would be fair to suggest that none of the evidence from Vindolanda securely places the Tungrians there after the 130s. However, a small building stone with the initials COH I TV (*cohors I Tungrorum*) can be seen in the south cross-wall of the fort's granary. The stone has been reused – it is placed upside down and from its position it shows building work by the Tungrians before the first rebuilding of the granary. Unfortunately, although the granary is amongst the best preserved buildings on the fort, there is very little secure dating evidence and all that can be deduced is that the inscription should date before the major modifications to the granaries, probably at the end of the second century. At present this is the best evidence to suggest any garrison before the late second century, but it does have the advantage in that it allows for a direct move from the earlier Stanegate garrison at Vindolanda up to the new forts on Hadrian's Wall itself. The fort at Housesteads shows no obvious signs of abandonment during the occupation of the Antonine Wall and an inscription of soldiers from the Second Legion 'on garrison duty' may be evidence of a caretaker garrison at this time (RIB 1583).

As an example of the complications of matching known units with the physical remains of forts when the First Tungrians next appear in the epigraphic record at Castlecarey in AD 142 as part of the garrison of the Antonine Wall they are thought to have returned to milliary strength. However it seems unlikely that the full regiment was in occupation at this fort since the total area is only 1.4 hectares (3.5acres) and therefore only a detachment of the First Tungrians are more likely to have been in garrison. By the beginning of the third century AD, the First Tungrians were certainly at Housesteads in full strength and nine altars from this period have been found recording dedications by the commanding officer (*praefecti*) on behalf of the unit. Many of these are dedicated to the Roman gods such as Hercules and Jupiter the Best and Greatest, others combine Roman deities with local cults. Most unusual is an inscription from the time of the emperor Septimius Severus, concerning an oracle of Apollo from Claros in western Turkey. Similar references to the oracle at that time are known from north Africa, Sardinia and Dalmatia (modern Croatia) (RIB 1579). No inscriptions survive from after AD 300 and the principal evidence for the garrison of Hadrian's Wall comes from the *Notitia Dignitatum*, army lists derived from an early fifth-century document, at a time when the British provinces no longer formed a part of the western Roman empire. The list for the Wall, beginning with the descriptive prefix of *Item per lineam valli*, 'Also along the line of the Wall', records the First Tungrians still at Housesteads, a remarkable continuity over nearly three centuries. Such continuity is rare on many of the frontiers of the Roman empire like the Rhine and the upper Danube which were disrupted by barbarian invasions. But elsewhere those more stable frontiers such as Cappadocia (eastern Turkey) reveal a similar pattern of continuity.

In the early third century, the garrison at Housesteads was supplemented by one or perhaps two units of German irregulars: *Cuneus Frisiorum*, possibly a cavalry formation termed a 'wedge' of Frisians. They were recruited from outside the Roman empire from the coastlands of eastern Holland and Germany. The

*34* Arch from the shrine of Mars Thincsus. With the inscribed pillar (*35*), this forms part of a temple dedicated in the third century by Frisian soldiers to the god Mars Thincsus and his attendants the Alaisiagae. The relief sculpture on the arch shows the warrior god with a goose at his feet, flanked on either side by cupids holding torches, symbols of victory. These stones and an inscription were found in 1883-84 on the north slope of Chapel Hill and were part of a large shrine including the visible Roman well. It is likely that the pillar and arch framed the apsidal sanctuary or the entrance of the temple. *Chesters Museum; English Heritage*

*35 Left* Inscribed pillar dedicated to Mars Thincsus, the two Alaisiagae and the Numen Augusti. This supported the right side of the arch (*36*), and the matching pillar has not yet been found. The dedication to the Germanic god of war, Mars Thincsus, is uncommon in Britain and is connected to the garrison of Frisians in the third century. The people writing the dedication identified themselves on the inscription as citizens of Tuihante, which survives as the place name Twente, in north-east Holland. The Alaisiagae were female attendants of the war god and are named here as Beda and Fimilena, another inscription identifies them as Boudihillia and Friagabis – the Valkyries of later German mythology. *Chesters Museum; English Heritage*

*36 Right* An altar dedicated to the god Silvanus Cocidius by Q. Florius Maternus, commanding officer of the First Cohort of Tungrians. Maternus' family are thought to have come from Colchester. The name of the god combines a Roman deity (Silvanus) with a native one (Cocidius), a common Roman feature of tolerant paganism in Roman Britain. *Chesters Museum; English Heritage*

Frisians built a temple to their native gods, *Mars Thinscus* and the *Aliagasai*, on the north flank of Chapel Hill, with altars dedicated before AD 235, in the reign of Alexander Severus (RIB 1594) *(34, 35)*. Another group of Germans can be identified on one of these altars as *numerus Hnaudufridi*, meaning simply 'Notfried's Own', bearing the name of its commander or tribal chief who raised it, like early regiments of Highlanders in the British army. These are probably one and the same unit identified as a *cuneus* in its official title and a *numerus* by the name of its leader. Reinforcements of irregular *numeri* are found at a number of forts on the northern frontier in the third century, but they rarely survive in the later army lists.

The officer commanding the First Tungrians held the rank of prefect. Such men came from the equestrian order in Roman society and formed the core of the provincial elite throughout the empire. Until the later third century it was usual for many of these men to spend part of their careers in public service, both civil and military. The names of five prefects are known from dedications preserved on altars. All carry the three names which were usual for men of this rank, by coincidence the first name of four of the five is Quintus, fifth child. Two men may have come from British families: the family of *Aelius Modestus* and that of *Quintus Florius Maternus (36)* who may have been related to the family of the *Florii* from Colchester, one of the oldest Roman towns in Britain. The origin of two of the others cannot be ascertained, but an altar to *Desidienus Aemilianus* in AD 258 (RIB 1589) records a family name known from Etruria in central Italy and also on the coast of Dalmatia (Croatia).

Although the Tungrians were originally recruited from their native territory, by the time they garrisoned Housesteads, many of the new soldiers were recruited in Britain. The evidence for this is largely based on surviving personal names, but explicitly British names are rare. Many soldiers adopted Roman names which effectively conceals their place of origin but this was an important step in the process of becoming Roman, since if a recruit survived his 25 years' service he and his family became full Roman citizens. An example of this is *Aurelius Victor* who set up an altar to the *Veteres* (RIB 1605). Most of the Romanised names are thought to represent native British recruits, but of the few surviving names from Housesteads many are German in origin. These may be associated with either the Tungrians or the Frisians. Two of the dedications from the altars devoted to *Mars Thinscus* specifies tribesmen from (*cives Tuihanti*) normally identified with Twente in eastern Holland (RIB 1593, 1594)[4]. An inscribed list of names of men and one woman, probably for a burial club, records that they are from south-west Germany (RIB 1620). The process of Romanisation can be seen, as the fathers' names or patronymics are Germanic but the successors are of a standard Roman form (*Delfinus* son of *Rautio*). A tombstone of *Hurmius*, a soldier of the First Tungrians, records the father's name as *Leubasmus*, which is probably German in origin and illustrates the same process (RIB 1619) of recruits of German origin joining the Roman army and taking Roman names.

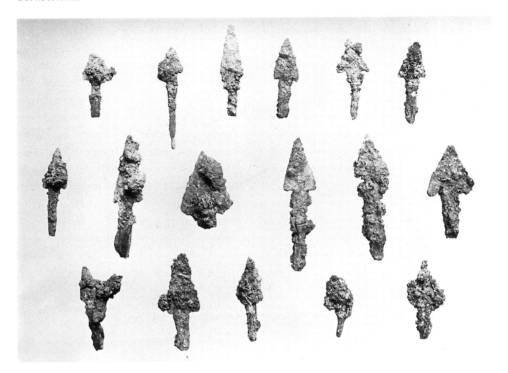

*37* Arrowheads found in the excavation of the headquarters buildings in 1898. The earlier auxiliary garrison was armed with swords and spears; archery came to have a greater significance later in the Roman period. *Hadrian's Wall Archive*

But this was not always the case, as two recent discoveries show. A potsherd from one of the flat-bottomed coarse-ware dishes Roman soldiers used as mess-tins had the owner's name, *Neuto*, scratched on the base. This name can only be paralleled in *Tungria* itself yet the pot can be dated to the late second or third century AD (*Britannia* 1983, 349, n 63). It appears to show that the regiment retained some level of ethnic identity more than a century away from its homeland. This could be a family tradition, but it more likely demonstrates some level of continued recruitment from Germany and the regiment's homeland, also indicated by the name A]maudio (RIB 2401.9). Another fragmentary name scratched on the side of a samian bowl dating from the later second century has been interpreted as deriving from the name of a Tungrian god, *Vanauns* (RIB 2501.829), also known from the fort at Castlesteads, where the Second cohort of Tungrians were stationed (RIB 1991).

This sample of non-Roman names is too small to base any firm conclusions about the continuing connections between ethnic units and their original recruiting grounds. However, it is possible to question some of the current views which presume that most infantry and cavalry auxiliaries will have recruited from within the province, from Housesteads and one or two other forts on the Wall garrisons. There are signs that certain units maintained close links with their native peoples into the third century. Details of auxiliary recruitment remain obscure and some soldiers clearly followed their fathers as sons of the regiment, while others were British in origin. But in the north it would appear that the native population remained at the least indifferent to the benefits of Roman rule and, possibly were actively hostile to the army of occupation. This means that recruitment from the immediate vicinity of the Wall garrisons, certainly before the fourth century, is unlikely, and that links with more distant recruiting grounds, both within and beyond the province of Britain, continued. The Romans, like later colonial powers, were not blind to the manpower resource of warlike highland tribes but they raised irregular units to serve away from their native territories, so that the *numeri Brittonum* (British units) served in southern Germany, while the Frisians and other Germans from the fringes of the empire were stationed at Housesteads and other forts in northern Britain.


## BUILDING HISTORY AFTER HADRIAN

It is possible to trace the history of the northern frontier in outline from the accounts of ancient historians, but these sources are fragmentary and the viewpoint is from the Roman and not the provincial angle. Relatively few barbarian invasions are recorded and their extent and location is frequently unclear from the sources. The principal events were at the end of the second century and in AD 367 and in the past, archaeologists have used these dates to establish the structural chronology of the forts and the Wall. Excavations at Housesteads have failed to find evidence for barbarian destruction at any period and it is difficult to relate the history of the fort to any such events. It is more fruitful to recognize that at certain periods there was imperial concern for and patronage of the frontier, best demonstrated by surviving building inscriptions.

On the death of Hadrian, Roman armies once more advanced in to Scotland and in AD 142 began construction of a new frontier, the Antonine Wall. Antoninus Pius seemed to be have been emulating Hadrian's 'victory by construction', but it was only occupied for two decades until about AD 162, when Hadrian's Wall was once more occupied in force. A fragmentary building inscription of the later second century found at Housesteads indicates rebuilding at this period and, on Hadrian's Wall there is archaeological evidence for contemporary rebuilding at Sycamore Gap.

The early third century witnessed the beginning of a major programme of building under Septimius Severus and his successors throughout the north of England. Much of Hadrian's Wall underwent restoration at this time and many of the forts were also refurbished. A Severan inscription from Housesteads records works on the *praetorium* (commandant's house) and another fragment of the same emperor, found reused in the fourth-century kitchen of that building, could relate to either the headquarters, granary or hospital, all of which can be seen to have been rebuilt after the Hadrianic period, but before the fourth century. It is salutary to recognise that after 150 years of excavation, many of the major buildings cannot be dated with certainty, so that much of the structural chronology must remain relative, rather than exact.

In the barracks in the third century there was little change, but the most radical alterations occurred between the *intervallum* street and the fort wall. In many places the rampart bank was removed and, against the north-east curtain workshops were set up. Similar changes can be recognised elsewhere, but the precise function of these buildings is not known.

# 6

# CIVILIANS

Just when you think you are at the world's end, you see a smoke from East to West as far as the eye can turn, and then under it as far as the eye can stretch, houses and temples, shops and theatres, barracks and granaries, trickling along like dice behind – always behind – one long, low, rising and falling, and hiding and showing line of towers. And that is the Wall!

But the Wall itself is not more wonderful than the town behind it. Long ago there were great ramparts and ditches on the South side, and no one was allowed to build there. Now the ramparts are partly pulled down and built over, from end to end of the Wall; making a thin town eighty miles long. Think of it! One roaring, rioting, cock-fighting, wolf-baiting, horse-racing town from Ituna in the West to Segedunum on the cold eastern beach! On the one side heather, woods and ruins where the Picts hide, and on the other, a vast town – long like a snake. Yes, like a snake basking beside a warm wall!

The quotations above are part of the description by the Centurion Parsenius in Rudyard Kipling's *Puck of Pooks Hill*. If it exaggerates and over-colours some of the details of the Wall, the forts and their garrisons, it evokes a powerful image of a special world created by the Roman army over two centuries. Kipling's view was obviously conditioned by his personal experience of the armies and frontiers of British India, but he was able to convey more than just the barren structures of Roman builders. Parsenius described a frontier world almost as different and distinct from the villas and towns of southern Britain, as the land of 'heather, woods and ruins' to the north. Kipling identified the narrow corridor of a Roman military world, with its own special sort of *Romanitas* or Romanness *(38)*. This was a classical culture articulated by the army in which the forts were images of urban civilisation and the Wall may be understood to represent the fortifications of a city which symbolised the empire itself. It is precisely the same imagery used by a Roman rhetorician, Aelius Aristides, to describe the empire of the second century AD.

But the story-teller was naturally drawn to the more colourful life beyond the confines of the military camps, the 'vast town – long like a snake, and wicked like

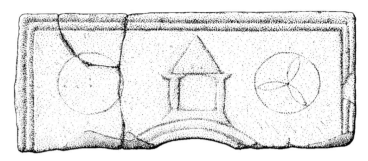

*38* Upper fragment of an arched window head. The central decoration shows the entrance to a shrine flanked by two columns surmounted by a triangular pediment. The circular decoration on either side was unfinished. *Drawn by Richard Annis*

a snake'. He exaggerated its extent, for the settlements outside the forts were quite small, more like piglets suckling around a recumbent sow than an unending, sinuous line of the story-book. And in any case by the late fourth century, when Kipling's story is set, few settlements survived outside the confines of the forts. But the evidence that does survive from the civil settlement at Housesteads, mainly discovered in the 1930s, confirmed in some ways the colourful picture of the life of the rough and venal soldiery.

At Housesteads, as at most forts, it is easier to recognise the presence of the military than of the civilian. The formal layout and exact boundaries of the fort clearly defined it from the country around. Outside it the stone buildings of the civil settlement are aligned on the existing pattern of roads leading along the Wall and southwards to the Stanegate at Vindolanda and Grindon. The settlement focuses on the east, south and west gates of the fort and straggles down to the south as far as, and over the course of, the *Vallum*. As with most extra-mural settlements along the Wall, the limits of occupation are ill defined, and the formal, nucleated settlement seems to peter out among the terraced fields on the fertile limestone soils.

But this was not the end of the Roman presence, for at the foot of the slope is the outcrop of limestone known as Chapel Hill, on and around which many of the stone altars were found. It was clearly a religious centre with temples to *Mars Thinscus* and Jupiter and a little along the ridge to the west, a small *Mithraeum* (shrine of Mithras) *(39* and *68)*. Sculptures of other gods and goddesses, especially the *Matres* or Mother Goddesses, were found in the field over towards the Knag Burn and it has been suggested, but never proved, that there was another temple there. The possible spot is marked by a large column drum, still visible in the long grass, but this is just as likely to have rolled down the hill from the fort when stones were being robbed for the building of the Military Road in the eighteenth century or during the creation of the modern pattern of the field walls. Roman cemeteries were often located on the fringe of settlements and could be associated with these temples. In addition to altars, a number of tombstones and funerary sculptures were also found in the vicinity of Chapel Hill, indicating that this was one of the fort's cemeteries, but no surface remains can be recognised as at Great Chesters or

*39* A stone sculpture showing the birth of Mithras from an egg – the symbol of Eternal Time. The god is framed in an egg-shaped zodiac representing the cosmos. The Mithraic cult at Housesteads stressed his role as 'Lord of Ages', and the complex imagery of the statue suggest the sophisticated nature of the cult at Housesteads. The statue stood in front of the relief showing the ritual slaughter of the bull, the focal point of the Mithraic sanctuary. It would have been lit from behind.
*Museum of Antiquities*

High Rochester. An early antiquarian visitor, Dr Hunter, who came to Housesteads in 1702, was told by local people that 'within living memory of their fathers, they used to bury their dead there', and cautiously added, 'I dare not determine the point there'. In the nineteenth century it was recorded that: 'On draining the marsh (south and east of Chapel Hill) a few years ago, considerable quantities of human bonework were found.' Other tombs may have lined the Military Way and other roads leading from the fort.

THE *VICUS*

Civil settlements or *vici* are found outside most of the Roman forts in Britain *(40)*. The term *vicus* (plural *vici*) is a Latin legal term denoting a settlement with an independent council, but lower in status than a fully developed town. Most of the so-called 'small towns' of Roman Britain are correctly termed *vici*, although the word is more commonly applied to those settlements associated with forts. A fragmentary dedication from Housesteads with the letters D VICA... can be completed as *D (ecreto) VICA (anorum)* 'by decree of the villagers', showing that at Housesteads there was a formally established settlement with the status of a *vicus (41)*.

Only those forts in remote or hostile situations such as High Rochester on Dere Street show no evidence for settlements outside the gates and *vici* are known from forts which were only briefly occupied. It seems likely that the *vici* were deliberately created rather than just growing up over a period of time. Many questions, however, remain about the origins, function and fate of these settlements. They are less easily defined than the forts themselves and the diversity of

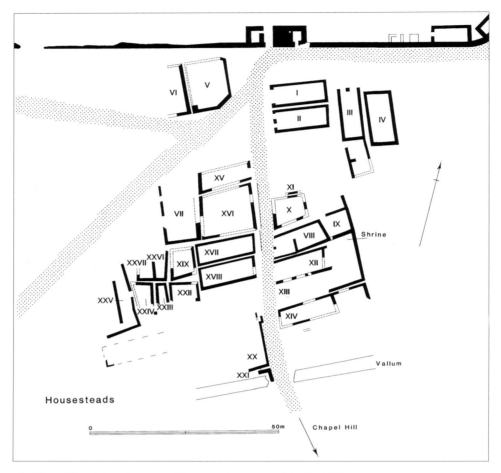

*40* Plan of the civil settlement at Housesteads, excavated in the 1930s

layout and buildings have made them less susceptible to the rather formal investigations characteristic of Roman military studies.

Why should there be buildings outside forts? Armies rarely march alone and frequent references from Roman writers mention camp followers and soldiers' servants and slaves. The numbers of these were substantial, especially in the legions and the cavalry regiments, although their presence is rarely considered in the complex calculations of the total numbers occupying forts and fortresses. Many were of a low social status so that their presence is very rarely reflected in tombstones or other epigraphic sources. The freedman Victor, who was commemorated by an elaborate tombstone from South Shields, constitutes the very tip of a social iceberg, only revealed by one who 'made good' in frontier society. These servants and slaves, however, had an official status in the Roman army; others, like the 'lady entertainers', known from graffiti surviving at the Euphrates' fort of Dura Europus in Syria, were a part of military life rarely visible in documentary or other sources.

*41* Fragmentary inscription of 'the decree of the villagers or *vicani*'; important evidence for the independent organisation of the community outside the fort. On the right is a small relief of Genius or 'the spirit of the place'. Another sculpture was found in the fill of the *Vallum*, immediately south of the *vicus*, and showed Mercury, the patron of merchants and thieves. *Hadrian's Wall Archive*

Who else might have formed the ready-made population of the *vicus*? Part of a soldier's pay was in cash – some of this was saved but there must have always have been a small surplus available for entertainment and other purchases. So amongst those who follow the army can be included the traders and merchants, some who settled in the settlements, others who were itinerant. These were the men who handled the supplies of pottery, who ordered the oil, fish sauce and olives from the western Mediterranean and, who supplied the wide range of perishable goods for the army on the Wall. One writing tablet from Vindolanda describes in detail the dispatch and transactions concerning a consignment of hides sent up from Catterick. The individuals are named but it is not clear whether they were soldiers or merchants – perhaps there was a second-century Sergeant Bilko at work in Vindolanda. At Housesteads and other *vici* it is these merchants who boosted the internal economy of the Wall forts and who were perhaps the occupiers of the large stone houses in front of the South gate.

The best-known part of the *vicus* at Housesteads is located south of the fort. Some structures were uncovered in the nineteenth century, but most of the excavations were carried out in the 1930s. A total of 26 buildings have been excavated or traced, although only six remain on display *(40)*. The largest and most unusual building is 5, immediately west of the south gate: the south-east angle was constructed to fit in with the pre-existing road leading to Vindolanda. The surviving walls are of large blockwork, rare in the buildings of the fort or *vicus*. It has been suggested that this was the residence of the *Beneficarius Consularis*, a representative of the imperial governor who was responsible for supervising transport and roads. One such official, *Litorius Pacatianus*, is known from an altar in the Mithraeum, but there is no reason to associate him with this building. The interior has been robbed out and no details survive.

Much of the *vicus* now visible and best known from the excavations of the 1930s is aligned with the road leading from the south gate to the crossing of the *Vallum*. This road in the second century must have always been one of the main roads leading from the fort providing the crucial access between the wall zone and the open territory south of the *Vallum*. The date when the *Vallum* was filled in at Housesteads is not known, but recent research at Birdoswald has suggested that this did not occur before AD 180. Once the *Vallum* was abandoned as a barrier it was then possible to build the new road leading south-west towards Vindolanda and it then makes sense to see this as the period when the stone-built strip-houses were constructed along the narrowed south road between south gate and the *Vallum*, contemporary also with the blocking of the east gateway of the south gate. These buildings with their short axis aligned onto the street are typical of *vicus* buildings found on the frontiers of north-western Europe, as well as in the Roman towns of Britain. Examples of this plan were built in both timber and stone and from the earlier excavations at Housesteads it is clear that in a number of instances limited remains of timber buildings preceded the stone structures, belonging to an earlier second-century phase of the *vicus*. Building 1 lies at a corner between the south road and the flagged 'bypass' road between the east and west gates. The long north wall of the building runs parallel to the fort wall and the building lies partly across the earlier road in line with the blocking of the east side of the south gate, suggesting that this layout of buildings beside the road dates from after the gate had been partly blocked. The house is divided into two rooms, a front room with a door and hearth, and a rear room with a basement below. In the later phase an oven was constructed over the basement. The basement was described as having been filled with a large quantity of pottery but this was never published. Among the other finds were dice – these were rather irregular in shape and were said to be 'loaded'. They may just be of rough local manufacture and whether it justifies its description as 'a gamblers' rendezvous' can be questioned. The oven in the back room is comparable to the ovens in the fort and suggests commercial production. Some of the latest coins known from the *vicus*, dating to no later than AD 320, were found in the final phase of this building, indicating that it may have continued in use after others were abandoned, probably because of its closeness to the fort.

Immediately to the south is building 2. It is similar in size and its entrance to the street consists of two stone sills with well-preserved slots, typical of the fronts of Roman shops closed with shutters. Shop fronts similar to this may be seen at Pompeii. The northern sill shows signs of the greatest wear. A coin of Severus dated to AD 197 was found in the mortar of the east wall and, below the floor were second-century coins of Hadrian and Commodus. The main stone structure can be dated to the early third century, although it was preceded by earlier structures.

Among the debris disturbed by seventeenth-century stone robbers, was a small statue of a Genius or guardian spirit for the owner and his family. This house, like its neighbour to the north, is pretty certain to have been a shop or tavern, with the owners' quarters at the rear and above. Many of the stone-built *vicus* buildings are of a similar size, 16m (52ft) long by 7m (23ft) wide and are much bigger than the soldiers' apartments in the barracks. The museum at Housesteads was built to the same ground plan as one of these stone buildings (8, the Murder House) and it gives a good idea of their size, many of which probably had upper floors.

Behind buildings 1 and 2 are two similar houses, facing the fort wall. House 3 opens on to the road so it may also have been a shop *(42)*. There was a store or stable at the south end, which is no longer visible. The stone building 4 was preceded by a timber cabin and, in later periods it was subdivided by a series of internal partitions. In the south part was a box furnace for metal working, and a similar furnace was found on the site of barrack VI within the fort. In the alley between buildings 3 and 4 was found a coin mould of a coin of Julia Domna, dated to AD 194-201. The furnace was presumably associated with counterfeiting, but whether these copies were semi-official or criminal is not clear. One of the problems faced by the distant Wall garrisons was the provision of official small change provided from Rome. At certain times this was in short supply or absent altogether and it seems likely that semi-official copies were made to provide small change for the soldiers and traders, a fact that reinforces the commercial activities associated with the *vicus*. A similar coin mould was also found in the well within the shrine of *Mars Thinscus* north of Chapel Hill. Continuing down the hill, the

*42* Photograph looking south across buildings 3 and 4 of the civil settlement. *Author*

buildings on the east side of the road, below building 2, were not investigated during the 1930s excavations, until numbers 10 and 8 were encountered. Building 8 is not the first building on the site and originally there was a longer house of which the east end 9 survived. House 8 was of the usual two-room arrangement with the outer flagging extended from the roadway into the front room, like buildings 1 and 2, an indication of public use as a shop or tavern. The inner room had an earth floor among which were found coins of the late third century. But at the east end a more gruesome and remarkable discovery awaited the excavators. Sealed below a clean deposit of clay were found the remains of two skeletons lying on the original floor. The more complete skeleton represented 'a tall, robust man of middle age' and in his ribs survived the point of a knife. The other skeleton was only fragmentary, but was thought to represent a slighter individual, possibly a woman. All Roman burials, apart from infants, were located outside the limits of settlement, so the discovery of these bones hidden below a back room floor must cause serious suspicion. In this case there can be no doubt that the man and women were murdered and that the crime was successfully concealed for seventeen centuries, the earliest incident of 'domestic violence' in British criminal history.

Of no less interest, in a yard immediately south of this house, was a domestic shrine set in a carefully built stone apse with a relief statue of three hooded figures *(43, 44)*. These depict the *Genii Cucullati*, hooded gods, who are grouped in a triad and resemble the hobgoblins or dwarfs of later legend. The relief was clearly made for this shrine since the sculptor misjudged the size and was forced to make

*43* Photograph of the excavations in 1933, showing the domestic shrine in the back yard of building IX. The relief of the *Genii Cucullati* was found in the small apse. *Hadrian's Wall Archive*

*44* Relief of the *Genii Cucullati* – hooded deities found in a shrine in the vicus and dateable to the early third century. They wear the hooded cape – *byrrus Britannicus* – famous as an export from Roman Britain. *Housesteads Museum; English Heritage*

the right hand figure slimmer than the other two. A votive offering of coins, dated from AD 220-29, was discovered under the relief and allows the shrine to be dated to the second quarter of the third century. The association of a sculpture with the shrine is important since normally these are found in the rubble of these buildings and the location and arrangements of domestic shrines rarely survive. Other sculptures from the *vicus* such as the *Genius* from house 2 and the figure of Mercury from the fill of the *Vallum*, help to show how religious life was not limited to the formal temples around Chapel Hill and the shrine within the Headquarters of the fort. The traces of at least three more buildings were seen south of house 8 towards the *Vallum*.

On the opposite side of the south road within the triangle created by the road leading towards Vindolanda and the south-west, excavation was more limited. A row of strip-houses (15–18) was located facing onto the road, but not investigated in detail. Building 16 was exceptionally large with a surface area of 44sq m (474sq ft) and connected with it was a well-built structure (7) which opened towards the west, on to the Vindolanda road. Its west wall was described as being 'of massive ashlar masonry, blocks measuring 6 feet by 2 feet 6 inches by 2 feet' (1.8m x 0.8m x 0.6m), which if correctly described is unique at Housesteads. The wall was pierced by two entrances, 1.5m (5ft) wide, and flagging extended from the outside pavement into the building. The scale and monumentality of it, like 5 by the south gate, strongly suggests that they both may have had an official function.

By contrast the limited diggings to the south of 7 revealed traces of houses of a very different character. These (19, 22-27) were often much smaller and were comparable in size to the 'chalets' in the fort. By comparison with the other *vicus* buildings they were of a rough and ready construction and were described by their excavators as 'nothing but hovels of the poorest description'. Pottery found in these buildings was noted as 'showing native characteristics' and it can be equated with a particular type of pottery, now termed 'Housesteads Ware'. This has been shown to be not of native manufacture as was suggested in the 1930s, but a type of pottery with very close similarities to the products of Frisia, the homeland of the *Cuneus Frisiorum* which formed part of the third-century garrison. A few sherds of this type are known from the excavations within the fort, but the largest quantity of Housesteads Ware was found outside the fort in the *vicus* excavations and, this strongly suggests that its users were accommodated in that area. Although the excavators in the 1930s were only able to sample a part of the total known area of the *vicus*, it is clear from the plan that there was a shift from the formal organisation along the south street to the more ramshackle structures revealed to the south-west. An explanation for this change could be that the Frisian unit was not stationed inside the fort, which the First Tungrians still occupied, but remained outside on the edge of the *vicus*. This theory can help explain the exceptional masonry reported from building 7, which may have served as the headquarters for the Frisians. Housesteads Ware is also known in quantities from Birdoswald and recent excavations have shown that the majority of the sherds were found in the group of timber buildings located over the filled-in course to the south of the south gate.[1]

Recent research on this very distinctive form of pottery has shown that it was manufactured in the area of Hadrian's Wall but that the particular forms of the vessels were derived from a ceramic tradition known in north-eastern Holland, the homeland of the Frisians. These soldiers were an irregular unit of cavalry under the command of their tribal leaders. A number of units of Frisians are known from the Hadrian's Wall garrisons in the mid-third century and the distribution of the distinctive pottery, to a large degree, matches the number of Frisian units known from epigraphic sources. What is especially interesting from the evidence from both Housesteads and Birdoswald is that the ceramic evidence indicates that these soldiers were stationed outside the main garrison in distinctive timber houses and that they also retained very characteristic aspects of their own indigenous material culture. This particular group of vessels represents only a part of the range of ceramics used in Frisia at this time, so there was clearly a conscious choice to reproduce these, but not other forms. Whether they had a particular culinary function is not known, however it is more likely they had a more specific cultural or symbolic function within the Frisian community. Further investigations are required in order to resolve these questions. But the evidence from the Frisian irregulars presents a different form of engagement with the Roman army and the patterns of daily life. Unlike the Tungrians and other peoples like the Dacians, who formed part of the standard structure of the frontier armies in the third century and who may have retained some of their earlier identity shown by a continuing contact with the original recruiting areas, on the one hand the newly recruited Frisians from outside the empire appear to have been treated differently. They were located outside the fort where we believe the majority of the garrison was housed, but they retained stronger aspects of their own ethnic identity seen in the Housesteads Ware and the timber housing. Yet the commanders of the unit were involved in the building and dedication of a temple below Chapel Hill, dedicated to a Frisian god melded with the Roman war god, *Mars Thinscus* (see below).

If a part of the *vicus* was occupied during the third century by a military unit, who built and who occupied the rest? The inscription referring to the *vicani* shows that there was a civil administration separate from the organisation of the garrison. The strip-houses are more substantially constructed than the barracks in the fort and they are regularly laid out. There is no reason for thinking that the land around the fort was not owned by the army and, it is quite likely that these houses were built by the army as well. These extra-mural buildings have produced some of the most vivid evidence for 'civilian' life in the frontier zone, certainly living up to the spirit of Kipling's 'roaring and rioting town'. Commercial activity is evident and the life-style is comparable to many of the towns of Roman Britain.

The ownership and tenure of the strip-houses remain enigmatic, but some of their occupants appear to have been better off than the ordinary soldiers. This raises once again the question of the soldiers and their dependants. Before the reign of Septimius Severus, serving soldiers were not allowed to marry. It is not clear what the significance of this was to their daily life since there were a number of different forms of marital status in the Roman world and, as in pre-modern rural Britain, marital ties were often fairly informal. The crucial question concerned the inheritance of Roman citizenship by the soldiers' children, hence the importance given to documents like the diplomas. What cannot be quantified is how many of these 'new Roman' citizens stayed in the frontier zone. As an indication some diplomas are known from the frontier, notably recent ones discovered from Vindolanda and Ravenglass on the Cumbrian coast, whereas many others have been found in the more distant recruiting grounds elsewhere in the empire. Therefore a proportion of *vicani* may well have come down from the descendents from the garrison, but we need to be aware of merchants, imperial officials and others as the occupants of the extensive strip-houses. It is less likely that they served as married quarters for serving soldiers, although evidence from papyri in Egypt suggests that some soldiers were more civilian than military in their occupations.

The whole question of married quarters in Roman forts is misleading and results from the application of late twentieth-century European values to a very different culture. Images of the family life of the garrison might allow the modern visitor to empathise with the foreign conquerors who built the Wall and relished hot baths, but what mattered to a Roman commander was that his men could fight efficiently and conquer and resist an enemy. Their welfare was not incidental as the provision of baths and hospitals attests, but all else was irrelevant. Until the twentieth century, few armies made any provision for married soldiers and their families. Soldiers' women were at the best tolerated: in the 1780s at Fort George near Inverness, only one in every 100 soldiers was allowed to 'marry on the strength'. Little concession was given to privacy and the wives, and any children, received half-rations in exchange for domestic chores. There is little reason to suppose that the women and families of Roman auxiliaries were any better treated.

Some of the most direct evidence for women on the northern frontier derives from inscriptions and especially tombstones where women and children are specifically commemorated, or set up the memorials.[2] Despite the wealth of Latin inscriptions from Housesteads, tombstones are relatively poorly represented. Only six are known in total, of which one mentions women as part of a list of names, possibly a burial club, and another provides a fragment of a female name and there are no references to children. The rarity of tombstones can be explained by the continuing problem concerning the location of the cemeteries at Housesteads, but elsewhere women and some children are represented, as an example from Greatchesters, the next fort next along the Wall to the west. Eight inscriptions mentioning female names are known: two record young girls, and the remainder are adult women, including one who is the sister of a soldier, in itself suggesting some local recruitment.

## THE ROMAN LANDSCAPE

A Roman fort presents a clearly defined and structured space, beyond its immediate limits at Housesteads and similar civil settlements, the main areas of settlement were like a ribbon development on the major roads leading out from the fort *(45)*. The extra-mural settlement, which as we have seen combined civil and military elements, provided an interface between the military garrison and the world beyond. The extent to which the *vici* created distinctive frontier communities remains a matter of continuing debate and research amongst archaeologists and historians. One particular issue is the extent to which the *vici* acted as a vehicle for the acquisition of Roman ways by the British population beyond the Romanised settlements. The two communities may have lived side by side, indeed as we shall see, within sight of one another, but in practice the northern tribes, unlike their counterparts in southern Britain, displayed little interest in acquiring the Roman ways.

A similar pattern of emerges from the study of the very extensive field archaeology surviving beyond the fort and the immediate stone-built extra-mural settlement. In the modern fields to the east, south and west of the fort, is one of the best preserved archaeological landscapes with a very complicated sequence of earthworks representing differing patterns of land-use over two millennia. Today it appears empty apart from sheep and visitors and a network of field walls neatly divides it, hardly a century old. Yet the man-made landscape around the fort has evolved over a long period of time. Different patterns of land-use demonstrate the many stages in its creation, so that in places the Roman changes are masked by later field systems *(46 and 66)*.

The earliest traces of Roman management of the land outside the fort were recently found in a small excavation close to the Museum. This allowed a glimpse

*45* Air photograph showing Housesteads and the remains of ancient fields and the *vicus* from the west. Note the broad line of the *Vallum* approaching the fort from the east of the Knag Burn wood and the way that the line is overlain by later fieldworks south of the fort and to the west. To the west of the west gate a sequence of Roman rectangular enclosures is visible aligned with the Military Way; compare with the plan (*66*). ©*Tim Gates, 1992*

at the pattern of earlier fields before the creation of the terraces, as well as providing conclusive evidence that the system of terraces was Roman in date. The earliest element found was traces of gullies and temporary enclosures of Roman date, followed by a pit filled with domestic rubbish dateable to the mid-second century AD. The line of a fence had crossed the filled pit before the radical creation of terraces with stone retaining walls running east to west across the hillside. These early enclosures were located nearly 100m from the south-west corner of the fort and the quantity of rubbish suggests that there was occupation of some significance in the vicinity, since it is unlikely to have been brought from the fort. The most likely land-use was as small paddocks for animals or possibly for arable use. No plough marks were noted in the subsoil from these excavations, although traces of pre-fort cultivation have been identified from beneath the barrack XIII. Small fields located on the north-east side of the fort have been

*46* View of the fields south of Housesteads, *c.*1920. Two quite distinct systems can be seen. The first, an extensive system of terraces with stone retaining walls, belong to the Roman period and was possibly reutilised in the twelfth and thirteenth centuries. Such a system would be used at a time when it was important to retain water in the soil – a period of climatic optimum. The alternative and opposite field pattern can be seen to be running down the slope. These are clearly secondary and later than the terraces, running from left to right on the photograph, and were employed to assist with the drainage of the soil, at times of excessive moisture such as 'the Little Ice Age', from the fourteenth to eighteenth centuries. *Hadrian's Wall Archive*

interpreted as possibly of pre-Roman date, suggesting that the hill-top and its flanks was the centre for a pre-Roman iron age settlement. An intensive air survey recently undertaken by Tim Gates to the north and south of the Wall in the central sector, has revealed a very complex set of early field systems termed 'cord rigg', a system of small-field arable cultivation current in both the pre-Roman and Roman Iron Age. In some instances it is quite clear from these photographs that Roman activity overlies the earlier cultivation, whereas as elsewhere the fields seem to be contemporary with the Roman period occupation.

The other evidence for early Roman activity outside the fort has been identi-fied at Chapel Hill, where there are waterlogged deposits preserving occupation debris over one and a half metres deep on the north side close to the Roman well. This material includes pottery dated to the second century and it has often been suggested that the earliest civil settlement was in this area, excluded from the fort by the *Vallum*. The remains of the well can still be seen amongst a clump of nettles and thorns and the spring was collected in a rectangular tank about 1.35m (4ft 6in) deep. Excavations in 1960 by Robin Birley (shortly before he turned his attention to work at Vindolanda) revealed that the well was enclosed within a D-shaped enclosure, with its apse pointing to the north. Stone-built structures were also uncovered to the east of the well and shrine and another stone building was partly investigated with evidence that it was later built over by a circular building. The sequence of buildings here has recently been re-interpreted by Alan Rushworth who suggests the apsidal building was the shrine of the Germanic god *Mars Thinscus*, originally excavated by John Clayton in 1883 with a limited record of the structural evidence. Amongst Clayton's finds were the decorated arch stone and an inscribed pilaster probably located in the entrance to the building *(34, 35)*. Two associated altars to the attendant gods the *Alaisiagae* (early versions of the Norse Valkyries) were found in 1920 to the west of the shrine. The shrine itself dates from the third century and was set up when the Frisian regiment formed part of the garrison at Housesteads and, coins from within the well date to the early fourth century. The other buildings north of Chapel Hill also underwent changes and the large stone hall east of the shrine and well, later included a wooden coffin set in a stone cist aligned from north to south —it was considered to date to the later third of fourth century. A curved wall constructed over a third building to the south of the hall has been suggested by Rushworth to be a round house, late Roman in date, but built in the native building tradition. Altogether the evidence from this part of the *vicus* suggests continuing occupation into the fourth century AD.

The different stages in the development of the *vicus* are poorly understood. The stone-built *vicus* has already been described, and in many places beneath the surviving structures traces were found of earlier timber buildings. How early these date is nowhere specified, for the question of the foundation date in this area did not concern past excavators, since for the most part they were convinced that the earliest settlement was located to the south of the *Vallum* ditch. It has been noted above that early pottery is known from the north side of Chapel Hill but it remains unclear why this should constitute the primary civilian settlement at the fort. Apart from Hadrian's Wall it is expected that the settlement was adjacent to the military garrison, since economically and perhaps socially the two were inextricably linked. It appears illogical that the Hadrianic Wall forts should have been thought to have been separated from their *vici*. Yet it is probably from Housesteads that the theory arose, in an attempt to explain the different locations of the settlements at the foot of the hill and close to the fort. In part these ideas may have arisen since it was presumed that there was a close link between the local population and the *vicani*. If, as we have seen, this appears not to have been the case, or at least the evidence remains equivocal, there seems little reason that the first extramural settlements were isolated away from the forts themselves. However what is clear from recent geophysical surveys of a number of Wall forts, including Halton Chesters, Birdoswald and Castlesteads, is that at their fullest extent the civil settlements were constructed over the site of the earlier *Vallum*. These surveys show the settlements at their fullest extent, which to judge from the recent evidence from Birdoswald, should be dated after the re-occupation of the Wall following the abandonment of the Antonine Wall.[3]

At Housesteads a simpler explanation might suggest that originally there were two distinct focuses to the extra-mural settlement. The first was located close to the well at Chapel Hill and grew to have a distinctly religious slant, possibly because of the common Celtic association of water spirits with wells and springs. Coventina's Well at Carrawburgh is an example of this phenomenon, although that lies within the *Vallum*. At the same time a good water supply may have been important for craft and other activities to encourage the settlement in this area. The second focus for the settlement must have been around the fort gates and this is represented by the timber phases located below some of the stone strip-houses.

The construction of the settlement in stone was a major redevelopment and probably forms part of the wider reorganisation of the landscape when the terraces were built in the later second century, when the *Vallum* no figured as a barrier to the south. This development will have significantly increased the area of land available for growing arable crops and, at the same time it will have ensured that dispersed settlement became concentrated closer to the fort. This could explain why the terraces stop to the east of the buildings beside the south road as this area became a focus for part of that settlement. The modern Museum marks the upper limit of the terraces and to the west of the fort, above it and as far as the Wall, there is a patchwork of enclosures, some of which are aligned with the Military Way from the west gate and are therefore of Roman date *(colour plates 1* and *2)*. These could be either allotments or stockyards; no dwellings can be recognised among them. The outline of buildings can however be traced outside the east gate beside the Military Way, but other remains on the south-east flanks of the fort are obscured by Roman and more recent agriculture. Once the *vicus* declined in the early fourth century, the land outside the walls will have become purely agricultural.

Going beyond the agricultural works, the cemeteries and temples of the Roman settlement recent air surveys, already noted, have shown that there were more extensive native settlements close to Wall and fort than previously thought. Beside the Stanegate on the ridge to the south, a complicated settlement has now been identified east of Crindledykes farm, three-quarters of a mile due south of the fort. The settlement is in direct view of the fort yet is only very recently that archaeologists have recognised it. Two other similar farmsteads are known, each one mile to the north, one on the crags beyond Broomlee lough and the other on the banks of Greenlee lough. The well-known site of Milking gap lies 1¼ miles due west between the *Vallum* and the Wall. These farmsteads to the north of the crags came as a surprise to some Roman archaeologists who had seen the Wall as a barrier in the central sector, but they represented a distribution of settlements in the marginal uplands, little different to the known patterns of Romano-British farmsteads from north Tyndale or Redesdale.

Unlike the Romans, these peoples have no voice for posterity and we can only speculate how they responded to the construction of the Wall when their land was requisitioned and the traditional patterns of herding and pasture were abruptly

*47 Right* The Knag Burn gate from the south-east. *Author*

*48 Below* Plan of Knag Burn Gate. The gateway was constructed in the third century after the north gate had gone out of use as a main entrance from north of Hadrian's Wall. There is no reason to believe that the gate was ever more than a military access through the Wall

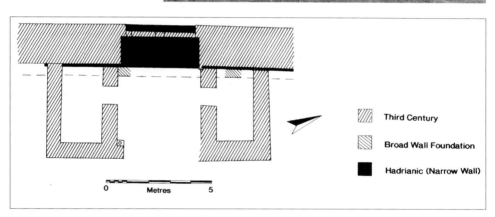

Third Century

Broad Wall Foundation

Hadrianic (Narrow Wall)

0   Metres   5

curtailed, first by the mural barrier and a few years later by the *Vallum*. Their experience of barrier walls was probably little different from the bitter lessons of Soviet-controlled Berlin and the Israeli West Bank. Hadrian's reign was marked by serious outbreaks of warfare in northern Britain, although the details remain obscure. It is still not known whether these were the reason for building the Wall, or alternatively whether their response caused the disruption in the building programme, evident especially in the central sector. Initially the British response would have been hostile, exactly the impression from the troublesome *Brittunculi* of the earlier Vindolanda tablets, although some historians interpret this text to refer to British recruits for the Roman army. But what evidence is there that the native population were later won over to Roman ways? If this is measured in material terms by the quantities of Roman artefacts found on native homesteads, both the south and north of the Wall, the impression is of very little contact. There are a few scraps of pottery, the odd glass bead, but little else, certainly when measured against contemporary rural settlements in the Midlands and south of Britain. Roman military sites are rich in iron tools yet rarely, if ever, are these found in native contexts. If this is the general impression, is it justified to assume that in time the natives formed a significant component in either the population of the *vici* or in recruitment to the garrisons of the forts? Fairs and markets are often considered to have been a part of frontier life, but whatever the natives received in exchange at these supposed events, has not entered the archaeological record in any quantity. The forts may have gathered in tribute from the native population but little trace survives.[4] *(47, 48)*.

# 7

# LATER ROMAN HOUSESTEADS CENTRAL BUILDINGS

The Roman Empire, in both the east and west, suffered major changes in the course of the third century, but this crisis in imperial security affected Britain less seriously than other parts of the empire in the west. On Hadrian's Wall there is no direct evidence from the archaeological record for enemy action in the late third century, but what stands out from a number of forts and milecastles are structural changes affecting the internal buildings and the defences. The evidence for such changes nowhere survives so clearly as at Housesteads and in many respects the remains which we see today derive from that period more than any earlier or later times. The precise date for alterations to a particular building is now often difficult to determine because of earlier archaeological activity but nonetheless it is possible to reconstruct a coherent pattern of change at the fort which can be dated to the years around AD 300. Recent discussions have concentrated on the transformation of the accommodation provided for the soldiers' barracks and on the implication this has for our understanding of late Roman garrisons on Hadrian's Wall and elsewhere in Britain and beyond. Before considering this structural evidence I should firstly like to consider the sole surviving epigraphic evidence for this period from Housesteads and the insight this gives us into imperial building activity in the fort.

In the Museum at Chesters, on a high ledge beside the proud fragments of Victory also from Housesteads, are the remains of one of the most richly ornamented inscriptions from the Roman Wall. It has received little attention, partly one suspects because of its late date and partly because the text is so fragmentary – only four letters survive. Despite this brevity it is possible to hazard a guess at least which emperors caused it to be erected. In the top left corner can be made out DD and below on the next line MA, which can be read as the plural of *Dominus* – master and *Maximiano*, a formula seen on the only other inscription of this date from Hadrian's Wall at Birdoswald:

*D(ominis) n(ostris) Dioc[letiano] et / M[axim]iano*
(To our lords Diocletian and Maximian….)

*49 Left* Reconstruction of the Tetrarchic inscription from Housesteads, based on the surviving fragments at the top left corner. The size of the inscription is based on lettering from the contemporary text at Birdoswald. The large size of the stone panel shows it came from a major new or restored building, probably the newly constructed stores or horrea at building XV. *Drawn by Alexander Rowntree*

*50 Right* The moulded base of a veranda pier from the second and third century barracks. Many were reused in later Roman buildings, including the Commandant's House. *Author, via the National Trust*

Diocletian and Maximian reigned as joint emperors (*Augusti*) between AD 286–305, each assisted by a junior colleague (*Caesar*), so that the Roman world was ruled by four emperors, and the period is known as the Tetrarchy, meaning four rulers in Greek *(49)*. The inscription from Birdoswald records the restoration of the Commanding Officer's house, the Headquarters and another building whose name can be restored to mean either a bath-house or a store for artillery. Although the Birdoswald stone was very worn as it had been reused for paving, it is clear that it was not as elaborately decorated as the fragments surviving from Housesteads.

The ornate decoration of the Housesteads fragments are unique in Britain and direct parallels are difficult to find from anywhere in the empire. In its detail the stone recalls the imperial imagery on monuments found in Rome and elsewhere. Recent accounts of the fourth-century garrisons on Hadrian's Wall and the late frontier armies have often drawn a picture of decline, reduction and loss of morale. Certainly there were changes in the internal organisation of forts from the later third century onwards but these transformations were not necessarily as negative as some commentators have assumed. At Housesteads in around AD 300 there is evidence for major building work demonstrated by the Tetrachic inscription described above. The question must be to try and establish which structure it refers to and it is necessary here to examine briefly all the buildings which are known to have been restored at about this time.

## COMMANDING OFFICER'S HOUSE (*praetorium*)

It is reasonable to assume that like the inscription from Birdoswald, the text concerned the official buildings or defences of the fort. The most difficult of these to interpret is the Commanding Officer's house, although this has suffered more than the two structures to the north from robbing and Clayton's clearance re-excavation allowed reinterpretation of many of the late features. This building is important for our understanding of the late garrison since any major changes in the status and wealth of the Commanding Officer could show in the structural remains. The various alterations to the original Hadrianic L-shaped building have already been discussed but there are clearly significant changes in the later period as well, best seen in the northern range *(27)*. At the east end was a kitchen (room 2), the raised oven on the west side was rebuilt using fragments of a dedicatory inscription of the early third century, similar to two others of this period from the fort. How long an inscription may be expected to have stood before reuse as a building stone is a recurring and ultimately insoluble question, but it seems unlikely that the oven was rebuilt before the end of third century. In the middle of the north range is a small room (5) with a well-preserved hypocaust.

Two of the pillars supporting the raised floor are reused veranda piers from the barracks *(50)*, which as we will see were rebuilt at the end of the third century, thus giving a *terminus post quem* ('the date after which') for the building of the heated room. The other pillars are monolithic oblong blocks, which were then waisted so that the ends swelled giving the effect of bases and capitals. Bricks are not used although one pillar is made up of thin sandstone slabs. Excavation in 1967-68 found 10 coins in the fill of the hypocaust, ranging in date from the late third century to the house of Valentinian I (364-78). The heated room originally had flues on the west, north and east side and, these were later carefully blocked. The furnace was located to the west at the east end of room 6 and a flue led through the west wall. Room 5 was probably a dining room for the *praetorium* and the coins and the structural changes suggest continuity of function until the last quarter of the fourth century. To the west were two rooms, 6 and 7, with an external doorway in the west wall. It has been suggested that these were separated from the rest of the building and, that this is an indication of the reduced status of the Commanding Officer in the later period but it is difficult to reconcile this view with the structural remains.

The most notable structures are the unusual floors constructed of long stone blocks, in places lying two courses deep. Similar blocks were also used as part of the flagging for the courtyard, and it is likely that the works were contemporary and fell within the same organisation. Originally this large block floor of room 6/7 was continuous and the undivided room extended across the two earlier rooms with a door to the west and probably another leading to the courtyard. The flags stop at the east end, indicating a separate enclosure for the *praefurnium* of the heated dining room (5) to the east, so it is likely that the furnace is earlier than the laying of this floor. No wall survives dividing the furnace from the room to the west but the change in floor level and the break in the flagging indicates a partition wall in this position. Later, the room 6/7 was subdivided and the dividing wall can be seen to be laid across the flags and a further layer of similar flags was added at this time. The door on the south side of 6 was then blocked, suggesting that it could then be entered from room 7. No dating evidence for these alterations was discovered but the similar use of long blocks in the courtyard suggests a similar period of construction. The use of these blocks deserves further comment, especially as they can be associated with other reused masonry in the courtyard, including an unfinished sculptured panel, probably an un-inscribed funerary monument, with two cupids supporting an ansate panel. Cupids are found on funerary monuments but alternatively they appear on imperial monuments, as symbols of Victory, such as the distance slabs on the Antonine Wall where they are considered to symbolise the prosperity of the empire. The Housesteads slab is unfinished and incomplete and it is not likely that a text was painted on the flat stone panel. It is dated, on stylistic grounds, to the second or third centuries.

Apart from this stone the flags included parts of stone water tanks and a broken window head but the vast majority of the surviving flags from the courtyard are identical to the long slabs from rooms 6 and 7, a job-lot acquired by the Commandant from a building in or around the fort.


## BUILDING XV

Building XV was long recognised as of special significance. Bosanquet noted that it was a conspicuous ruin and observed the buttresses on the north side. The small, later bath-house at the east end had been excavated by Hodgson in 1820 and will be considered later, and the three earlier structures have already been described. When building XV was excavated in 1962, a coin of AD 259-273 was found in the southern drain of the stable. Further excavations in 1981 at the east end, showed that this drain was sealed by the make-up for the large stone building and that this coin provided a *terminus post quem* of 259, or 'the date after which' for the construction. This was an important revision since on both stylistic and dating evidence it had been previously considered to be Severan (early third century) in date, and the structure became one of the only securely dated late Roman buildings in the fort.

The large stone building has overall dimensions of 49.5m by 10.8m (162ft x 35ft), similar in overall size to the two barracks, XIII and XIV to the north. Little more than two or three courses of stonework survive, but the walls display some of the grandest stonework of any of the internal buildings at Housesteads, certainly larger than the walls of the three central range buildings. The construction of the lowest courses consists of large blocks laid alternately as headers and stretchers, with little or no rubble fill. On the north side where it is best preserved the blocks are a little smaller, but similar methods are used with a rubble core. Many of the blocks have a distinctive cross-hatch dressing and there are small notches in the top of the blocks, used to help lever the stones in position. Such notches are rarely encountered except on the bridges of Hadrian's Wall. On the north side are seven buttresses, which are only bonded into the foundations, not the surviving wall above. The south wall has been much more extensively robbed and no trace of buttresses survive, but there is no reason to doubt their existence *(51)*.

Following the excavations in 1962 it was suggested that because no debris or rubble survived from the building the stone walls probably stood little higher than today and, the remainder was completed in timber. This seems unlikely and we can be certain that the unusually large worked blocks were taken for reuse; just as the more massive voussoirs of the neighbouring milecastle were taken to build kilns and walls in the neighbourhood. During these excavations it was clear that not only the walls but part of the flagged floor was also taken, although it survived better at the east end. Nothing is known of the roofing materials, which were probably of stone slates. The buttresses cannot have supported the walls of the building but were intended to carry a wide roof as is reconstructed for the granaries of the fort. Inside, the stone hall was flagged with sandstone laid on a thin layer of clean sand. Great care was taken to ensure that the interior floor was level from east to west, and at the east end there are deep deposits of tipped clay and rubble sealing the earlier sloping floors and even today the turf covering presents an unusually level sward on the Housesteads downs. At the east end, close to the area disturbed by the construction of the baths, a stone block set below the level of the flagstones with a socket 18cm (7in) square was found in 1981. No other blocks of this type had been observed in the 1962 excavations where the floors were more extensively disturbed by later reflagging and robbing. This block was positioned centrally across the building and is evidence for a row of central posts, presumably to support an upper floor, although it might be argued that two centuries of timber exploitation had exhausted supplies of suitable timbers. Further evidence for an upper floor comes from two post sockets located against the north wall. These were found 1.5m (5ft) apart and originally interpreted as part of a partition. How this could have functioned against the wall is unclear, but alternatively they may be the rear posts of a staircase for an upper floor. The building was entered from two sides, to the west and on to the *via principalis* by a door 1.5m (5ft) wide, and from the south and the *via praetoria* midway along the south side by a doorway 10ft wide. Carts or barrows could have used this entrance

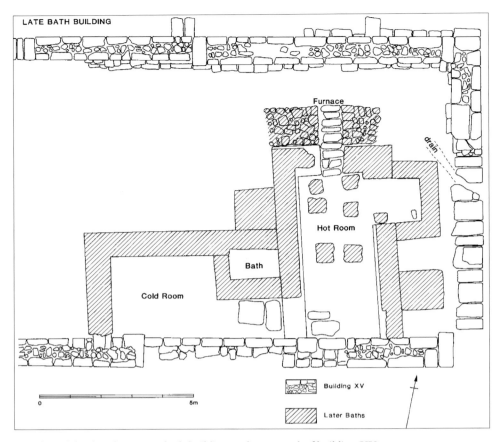

*51* Plan of the fourth-century bath building at the east end of building XV

and there are ruts in the wide threshold. The staircase suggested above would have been located 2.20m (7ft) south of this doorway, allowing carts access into the building and easy transfer to the upper floor. A number of late third- and fourth-century coins were recovered from the flagged floor.

The internal area of this building is 423sq m (4,550sq ft), that is 100sq m larger than the granaries at Housesteads before they were subdivided. Bosanquet was unclear about its function but the excavators in the 1960s considered it to be a stores building. Certainly when it was first constructed around AD 300 it was a two-storeyed, two-aisled stone hall with a main entrance on the *via preatoria* close to the main entrance of the fort. Unlike earlier granaries in forts there was no ventilation for the ground floor, but there does appear to be positive evidence for an upper floor serving this purpose, and other granaries at Birdoswald and Wallsend are known to have had solid or near-solid floors. Nevertheless it is better to refer to it as a storehouse rather than a granary, although the Latin word *horrea* means both.

GRANARIES *(horrea)*

Although these buildings were noted since the eighteenth century as the most prominent structure within the fort, it is ironic that we know least about its detailed chronology because of unsupervised clearance in the early 1930s. As a result all that is certain of the later history of this structure is a relative chronology based on observations of the surviving structure. If we can accept that the major alteration from a large single building to two parallel granaries occurred in the third century, it is possible to attribute later structural changes to the late Roman period. The north granary survives today as it was left after the second period changes and the absence of wear on the threshold has already been noted. A likely explanation for this preservation is that it was either abandoned or not repaired after a structural collapse, leaving it in the fourth century as a ruinous mass – the implications of this suggestion will be considered later. In the south half of the building by contrast a number of significant changes occurred. The south granary was divided in half by a cross wall, now partly obscured by the early medieval corn-drying kiln. In the west half the monolithic stone piers for the raised floor were cleared away, a few are left against the side walls and a narrow door was inserted in the east end of the south wall. It is not recorded if the west loading bay was blocked at this time. Unlike the other surviving external walls of the granary, no buttresses are seen on the south face, implying a rebuild, probably of Roman date. The floor of this room was flagged and the 1936 Guidebook of the site describes that 'a considerable amount of late pottery and the usual debris of occupation were found on them when they were opened up by the National Trust in 1931 and 1932'.

The east part of this building appears to have continued as a granary with a new entrance at the east end, approached by massive stone steps. The raised floor at this period was probably supported on sleeper walls, shown on the first complete plan of the fort made in 1898. Only the stone piers survive today. This would confirm Bosanquet's description of the floor supported on dwarf walls, built when the granary was halved in length and a new loading bay constructed. The overall size of this granary significantly reduced, making it comparable to granaries inserted into the headquarters building at Vindolanda, thought to date to the later fourth century. The implications of these changes for the size of the garrison will be discussed in the next chapter. Similar changes to the domestic occupation of part of the granaries are also seen in the building, identified as the hospital (*valetudinarium*). Late occupation in the hospital is represented by finds of fourth century pottery in the long north room – it too would seem to have lost its earlier public function.

## HEADQUARTERS BUILDING (*principia*)

The one building which can be expected to reveal major transformations in the life of the fort in the fourth century is the headquarters. Again we are faced with similar problems of earlier robbing and clearance, but many of Bosanquet's descriptions allow an interpretation of the changes which occurred. The main alteration to the appearance of the headquarters was the walling off of the porticoes in the third century *(52)*. The major structural change was in the south rooms of the *aedes*, rooms 8 and 9. The cross wall was removed and a new north-south wall replaced it. Associated with this was a drain cut in the south-west corner of the south wall. One explanation, based no doubt on similar modifications at Vindolanda, is that the wall and drain show the construction of a latrine, further evidence of the increased domestication of the *principia*. This seems altogether too elaborate and a more plausible interpretation is that these are staircase for an upper floor. Second floors are notoriously difficult to define in the archaeological record but at Housesteads, Bosanquet's remarkable discoveries at the north end of the *aedes*, provide convincing evidence for such a feature in the late Roman period and, his graphic description and discussion is worth quoting in detail:

> Rooms 11 and 12 were filled by a high mound which remained undisturbed not only when parts of the surrounding walls were removed in previous times, but ever since the *praetorium* (headquarters) fell into ruin. This mound contained more than the usual quantity of building stones, the usual mixture of broken slates, and one unusual element – a quantity of fallen flue tiles [...]. The evidence points to the existence of an upper storey. The flue tiles in room 12 extended in a line from east to west, starting from a point near the north-east angle: those in room 11 were scattered, but all lay in the northern half and most in the north-east quarter of the room. Round them was the clay in which they were bedded and soot shaken from them by their fall. They were black with smoke inside, and there can be no doubt that they had formed heating flues in the east wall of a room, forming an upper storey above 11 and 12. The furnace must have been placed on the solid platform outside 12. We can only conjecture that the missing southern part of it, which has been demolished for the sake of the large stones of which it was built, included a flight of steps and so supplied access to the upper floor. I have already referred to the coal and scoriae (slag) found in this corner of the court. The flags composing the top of the platform show marks of fire.

The lower floor in room 12 was simply flagged and access to the room above was facilitated because 12 was partly dug into the sloping hillside. On the lower floor were found the remains of stone slates fallen from the roof before the collapse of the walls and flue tiles, and below these was a mass of more than 800 iron objects, mostly arrowheads but also including an anvil, a pair of compasses, nails and a large hook *(37)*. Some of the nails retained the shape of the bag from which they had hung.

*1* An air photograph of the Whin Sill Crags with Peel Crags and Crag Lough in the centre. It shows the Whinstone escarpment which the Wall follows and the crests of sandstone ridges to the north and south. The line of the Military Way and Vallum are clearly defined. Housesteads is to the top of the photograph, south of Broomlea Lough. © *AirFotos*

*2* An air photograph of Housesteads from the west. The Whin Sill Crags and the line of Hadrian's Wall can be seen running to the east. To the right is the line of the Vallum and, at the bottom, the enclosures west of the fort are clearly visible. The line of the Military Way and an earlier road to the south-east can be seen beyond the wood. © *AirFotos*

*3* Reconstruction of the fort and civil settlement in the third century seen from the south-west. Note that much of the open ground west of the built external settlement was probably densely occupied. *Philip Corke, English Heritage*

*4* Reconstruction of turret 36B before the building of the fort. The foundations of the Broad Wall are shown leading up to the turret, while it is unclear how much of the turret was completed before the fort building began, this view provides a useful image of the standing turret and incomplete wall. *Philip Corke, English Heritage*

*5* Barrack XIII in the later second and third centuries. The soldiers are shown standing on the veranda in front of the entrance to the barrack rooms. The north-east angle tower and rampart can be seen at the top right of the image. *Philip Corke, English Heritage*

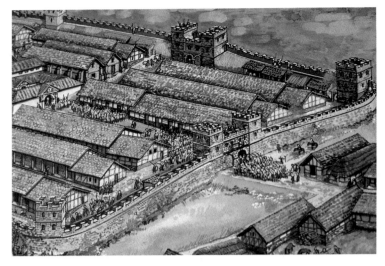

6 Reconstruction of the east side of the fort and the east gate from the south-east. Note the buildings constructed behind the north rampart as workshops in the third century. *Rena Gardiner, The National Trust*

7 Watercolour of the west gate by H.B. Richardson. These paintings formed the basis for many of the engravings in Collingwood-Bruce's *The Roman Wall*. They are now in the collection of the Laing Art Gallery. *Hadrian's Wall Archive*

8 Reconstruction of the north gate from the interior. Internal buildings have been omitted, the gate is shown with open towers, although evidence from the west gate at Housesteads suggests that at least the space over the gateways was roofed – see figure 15. *Philip Corke, English Heritage*

9 Reconstruction of the interior of the Housesteads latrines from the west. Unlike earlier reconstructions, this correctly shows the water flowing in an anti-clockwise direction. *Philip Corke, English Heritage*

10 Reconstruction of the interior of the commanding officer's house showing the Prefect in conversation with the senior centurion of the cohort. *Philip Corke, English Heritage*

11 Reconstruction of the interior courtyard of the hospital. In the fourth century this building was used for accommodation for the garrison. *Philip Corke, English Heritage*

*12* Reconstruction of the granary from the east. This shows the building in its first phase before later subdivisions; compare this view with figure 30, showing the building with two storeys. *Philip Corke, English Heritage*

*13* View of the fourth-century chalet phase of barrack XIV showing the individual units which had replaced the earlier barracks blocks. *Philip Corke, English Heritage*

*14* Reconstruction of the late sixteenth-century bastle house at the south gate. This was one of three fortified farmhouses built within the site of the fort in the late Tudor period. The bastle incorporated part of the south gate and the blocked Roman doorway is visible. *Philip Corke, English Heritage*

*15 Above left* The first season of excavations at Barrack XIII by students from Newcastle University in 1974. *Charles Daniels*

*16 Above right* View looking down on the central part of Barrack XIII from the west in 1977. *Charles Daniels*

*17 Right* The bath suite at the east end of building XV, showing the cold bath. *Author 1981*

*18 Right* A watercolour of Housesteads farm, c.1850. *Museum of Antiquities*

*19 Below* 'Building of the Roman Wall', a painting by William Bell Scott in 1850, from the central hall at Wallington, Northumberland. One of a series of paintings representing scenes from Northumbrian history – it is set on Hotbank Crags looking to the west. The Roman officer was modelled on John Clayton, owner of a substantial estate on Hadrian's Wall, including Housesteads and this sector of the Wall. At his feet, the sharp profile of John Collingwood Bruce looks towards the hostile natives. *The National Trust*

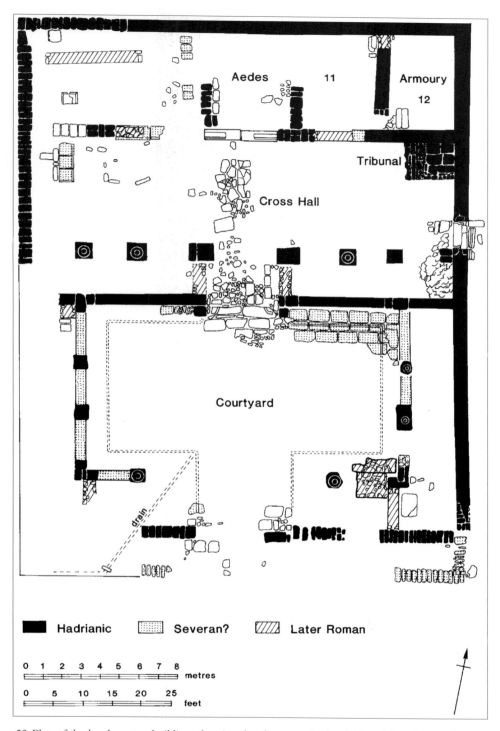

Aedes 11

Armoury 12

Tribunal

Cross Hall

Courtyard

drain

Hadrianic      Severan?      Later Roman

0 1 2 3 4 5 6 7 8
metres

0   5   10   15   20   25
feet

52 Plan of the headquarters building, showing the alterations in the third and fourth centuries

The arrowheads seem to have been arranged in bundles but almost all of the wooden shafts had rotted. The collapse of the upper walls and the deposition of the finds on to the hearth can dated after a coin of Constantine I from the floor of room 11 (elsewhere Bosanquet refers to this as a coin of Constantius). The lower room was apparently used as a workshop and weapons store, and above were more comfortable offices or domestic quarters. These arrangements are comparable to the late *principia* at Vindolanda where there is a heated room in a similar position, although that building seems to be newly built in the late third century. In the south room of the rear range where stairs were constructed, there is further evidence for domestic use from a moulded slab used as a hearth and the discovery of a pair of bronze tweezers were found on the late clay floor of the room.

The basilical cross-hall *(53)* was also altered at this time by the addition of short cross-walls across the width of the aisles immediately behind the door responds. There is evidence for rough flags in the central entranceway. In the south angle formed by the southern corner of the walls Bosanquet found the remains of a hearth and ashes set in the sheltered angle with pottery dated to the late third century. Another hearth lay across the hall to the west, once more using a reused moulded block. The addition of the 'wing-walls' behind the responds still allowed the double doors of the cross-hall to close, but a later addition of another wall to the north was probably added to support the lintel and roof of the entrance. In the outer court the closed-off porticoes were divided off the west ends.

Unlike the late Roman *principia* at Vindolanda, at Housesteads the headquarters building was not rebuilt but only modified. The central *aedes* seems to have remained the focus of the building, and the rooms to left and right conventionally interpreted as offices underwent a variety of changes, apparently including some form of roof conversion. If the normal reconstruction of the roof of this part of the *principia* is followed. The major difference is more hearths, but this could reflect no more than a change over from braziers, which leave little trace, to fireplaces. Pottery associated with these changes can be dated to the fourth century.


STOREHOUSES AND THE *ANNONA MILITARIS*


Having examined the remains of all four of the main 'official' buildings in the fort, we should return to the initial question which, if any, is to be connected with the Tetrarchic building inscription. The only new building is XV – all the others appear to have been modified, altered or reduced, even if the earlier function was retained. Building XV was a large structure, with stonework more massive than any earlier building. It has been interpreted as a storehouse since it differs radically from the contemporary barracks and other accommodation for officers and men. The late third century witnessed a major change in the nature of taxation in the Roman Empire in response to rampant inflation throughout much of the third century. The change was to collect all or part of revenue in kind a system known

*53* R.C. Bosanquet's excavations of the cross-hall of the headquarters building. Note the different construction phases visible. *Hadrian's Wall Archive*

as the *annona militaris*. How and if this system worked remains obscure, especially as there are still many coins in circulation in forts and other military sites. If the system was to work, new storehouses like tithe barns were needed both to collect and to redistribute food, equipment etc. The structural evidence for this is not well documented. The stores base at South Shields had become a normal fort by the early fourth century and it offers no comparisons. Some of the forts, both on the Roman Wall and to the north, seem to have an excessive number of granaries – see High Rochester and Chesters – but only Housesteads has a building such as this. One possible comparison may be drawn with granaries found in the north part of the Roman town at Corbridge, excavated before the First World War.

Comparative evidence is found in Continental Europe: from Germany where there are fortified granaries at Wilten, from Hungary at Tokod and elsewhere and from the lower Danube at Iatrus and Abritus (modern Bulgaria). Some of these buildings have external buttresses, but others are internally divided by two or more aisles like the building from Housesteads. It is unfortunate that the epigraphic record in the late empire becomes so fragmentary, since so few other inscriptions are known. We can however, suggest that the function of these storehouses was more than just to supply their own fort; they should be seen as part of a wider system, as distribution and collecting centres, thus explaining why the fort's old granaries were still required and why the dedicatory inscription was of a grandiosity unmatched by the contemporary text from Birdoswald.[1]

# 8

# LATER ROMAN HOUSESTEADS DEFENCES AND BARRACKS

Major changes occurred in the form and appearance of the defences and barracks at the end of the third century. For nearly 200 years there were 10 or more barracks in the fort and their basic plan remained unaltered, but in the last decades of the third century, probably at the same time that the new storehouse (XV) was built, the form of the barracks was radically changed and the fort's defences underwent major rebuilding.

A new design of barrack was created but significantly there was no radical change of location and these buildings occupied the same site as the earlier barracks. The main difference was in their external appearance for instead of a long roof running the full length of the barrack from east to west *(colour plate 5)*, each of the new barrack units had an individual roof with the ridge aligned across the axis of the former block, from north to south. Each row would have resembled a line of beach huts or 'chalets' – hence the name which has been given to them.

Traditional Roman barracks were communal and they were built for a specific unit of men, at Housesteads probably a century of around 80 infantrymen. The new order consisted of independent buildings, with a narrow alley between each chalet, so that one archaeologist coined the phrase 'chalet-alley-chalet' to describe the scheme. There was a shift from the communal order of the barracks, with the whole century accommodated beneath a single roof and with a centralised responsibility for the buildings' maintenance, to a series of new independent dwellings which once built, show evidence for separate choice in their maintenance and development.

## HOUSESTEADS AND FOURTH–CENTURY BARRACKS

The pattern of late Roman chalet-barracks can be recognised throughout the fort at Housesteads as recorded in Bosanquet's plan of the 1898 excavations. Pairs of parallel walls, indicative of chalets, can be seen at all the barracks and show that each block was rebuilt to this design. They are also seen at the east end of building VII (located to the north of the granaries), showing that whatever had been its earlier function, it now served as accommodation. The process of conversion of

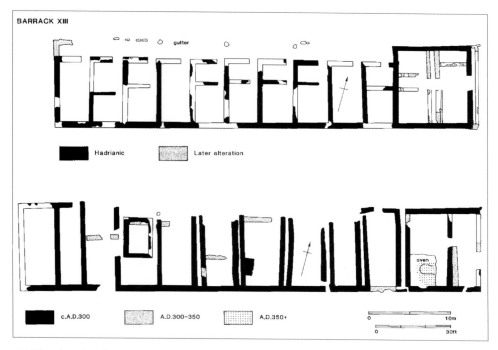

*54* Plan showing the structural changes in barrack XIII: (above) in the second and third centuries; (below) the fourth century alterations as a chalet-barracks

the barracks and their subsequent building history is best documented from the recent excavations of barracks XIII and XIV and of the defences between the north and east gates.

Both barracks XIII and XIV were conventional in plan *(54)*, although XIV underwent a major reconstruction soon after it was first built. The rebuilding of both blocks as chalets can be dated by coins and pottery to the end of the third century AD. The roofs and timber upper work of the barracks were demolished, but the rear walls, in both cases the south, were retained virtually intact, as were many of the dividing walls of the *contubernia* in barrack XIII which were reused in the new buildings.

The centurion's quarters of both barracks had undergone a number of alterations throughout the third century, but continued as distinct, larger units in the first period of reconstruction as chalets, including the provision of a latrine and a raised heated floor in XIII. At the west end of this block there was also a larger group of buildings, different from the chalets in between, with party walls and an open fronted room facing to the west. Altogether there are six independent chalets in block XIII. They vary slightly in length between 8m and 10m (26ft–33ft) and in width between 3.6m and 5.15m (12ft–17ft), with most falling in the range of 4.25m–4.65m (14ft–15ft). When first constructed, they did not have internal divisions and the north ends of the buildings were closed with either walls or

*55* A decorated string
course originally
positioned at the corner
of the gate towers.
*Author, the National Trust*

timber shutters. Many of the chalets had flagged floors, sometimes incorporating
the walls of the earlier *contubernia*. Most have hearths, although braziers using coal
or charcoal were also used. A feature of block XIII was the extensive re-use of
stonework from buildings in the fort. These stones included the decorated veranda
piers from the barrack phase and moulded string courses which probably derived
from the upper storeys of the fort's gates *(55)*. Similar stonework is also seen in the
repairs to the rampart, suggesting that the work was carried out at the same time.

Block XIV underwent similar changes. There was a central group of 7 chalets
with a larger unit replacing the centurion's apartments *(colour plate 13)*. Unlike XIII,
there was only a small room, possibly a workshop, at the west end. Many of these
chalets appear later to have been reduced in length and width, perhaps to accom-
modate an empty space between the chalet row and north wall of the storehouse
XV. An oven built in the large building at the east end indicates some communal
function and organisation. Later this structure was demolished and the space was
used as a hard-standing level with the *intervallum* street and the road to the north.
A large number of nails found on the road surface suggest that this was a deliberate
demolition and that the timbers were reused after the nails had been extracted.

In block XIII a number of minor modifications are seen throughout the fourth
century. Cross-walls were built creating new internal divisions, wood partitions
were added and there is evidence for new north walls. Large monolithic piers were
reused at the north end of one chalet to form a porch against the north-west wind.
At the east end, the former centurion's quarters, as in block XIV, passed into
communal use and there are two phases of horseshoe-shaped ovens, part of a group
of rooms opening eastwards on to the *intervallum* road. It is tempting to suggest
some continuity with the bakehouse which had served these two barracks before
the rebuilding of the rampart.

What conclusions can be drawn, if any, about the character and strength of the
garrison at Housesteads on the basis of these structural changes?[1] One clear distinc-

tion from the earlier barracks is that the chalets were never identical with one another. Each chalet displays an independent, if related, building history with its neighbours. Some have stone walls with doors set between wood jambs facing onto the street, while others have timber fronts and retain the evidence for wooden partitions. These differences represent individual choices, as if the occupants of each dwelling constituted a separate group. On the other hand, the reduction of the south ends of the chalets in block XIV can be interpreted as a communal decision, or one imposed by an outside authority, probably connected in some way with the storehouse to the south. Another instance of continuing communal use may be the ovens located at the east ends of both blocks.[1]

A modern analogy can be made with the changes in public housing in the 1980s and '90s. New central government policy has encouraged the sale of many council houses into private ownership. The responsibility for their maintenance has passed from a public body to individual owners. The effect of this privatisation on many former council estates has been to radically alter their appearance, with a variety of structural innovations, differing colour schemes and even stone cladding. Despite these changes however, in many cases the new owners remain the same; modifications in outward form and appearance reflect no significant alteration in the population, its livelihood or social structure, there is merely a transfer in tenure and responsibility for household maintenance. Some observers however, might argue that these apparently modest changes are witness to longer term social and economic transformations in British society.

The renewal of the barracks as a row of chalets could be interpreted therefore as little more than the necessary reconstruction needed by part-timbered buildings which had stood for nearly two centuries. The phrase 'collapsed through old age' is found on many Roman building inscriptions and serves as a reminder that Roman buildings required repair and renewal, even if the phrase itself can often have a rhetorical as well as a literal meaning. No building inscription is known from the forts of Hadrian's Wall referring to the rebuilding of barracks, but an inscription, datable to AD 255-60, records the rebuilding of a barrack from ground level at the legionary fortress of Caerleon.

Comparable changes in the plan of barrack buildings have been identified at other Wall forts such as Great Chesters, Wallsend, Birdoswald and the outpost fort at High Rochester. The archaeological evidence, principally from Housesteads, suggests that these changes occurred towards the end of the third century. At Vindolanda and South Shields, recent excavations have identified a different type of barrack arrangement, dating from the middle of the third century. This type of barrack shares some features in common with the chalet-barracks, notably the provision of six *contubernia* with a separate quarters for the centurion. Crucially the excavated examples from South Shields remain as a single communal unit throughout the fourth century and do not display any of the variety seen on chalet blocks.[2] The difference may be related to the location of the two forts behind the Wall, perhaps occupied by higher status garrisons in the fourth century.

An alternative explanation for the conversion of barracks has suggested that the 'chalets' represented family units occupied following the decline and abandonment of the civil settlement outside the fort. This interpretation has radical implications concerning the nature and size of the garrison at Housesteads, since it can be argued that if non-combatants now filled the fort the effective size of the garrison was thus radically reduced. If this pattern were to be repeated throughout the forts in northern Britain, it also has significant implications for the cost of maintaining and supplying the Roman garrisons in Britain. Before considering this problem in detail it is necessary to review the evidence for the reconstruction to the fort's defences and to assess briefly the changes in the later Roman army in Britain and beyond.

## THE LATE DEFENCES

Even a glancing look at the outside stonework of the fort wall at Housesteads shows how often it was repaired and reconstructed during the Roman occupation. The fort walls were relatively stable to the east and west – various sections still display a thin levelling course, probably dating from the Hadrianic building of the fort. Elsewhere, and especially at the corners and on the south and north sides where the walls were built on a slope with the weight of the rampart bank behind them, frequent and extensive repairs were needed.

The interior and exterior of the curtain wall were mostly cleared by John Clayton's labourers in the middle years of the nineteenth century, so that little stratigraphic evidence has survived. A recent excavation of a part of the exterior of the fort wall to the east of the north gate by the writer, together with the work in the north-east quadrant, has enabled the basic phases of construction to the fort wall to be summarised as follows:[3]

1   Hadrianic construction of the fort wall. The north and south sides show that there was a shallow construction trench for the footings of the wall and it not surprising that the wall proved to be unstable over the next three centuries.
2   Major repairs were carried out towards the end of the second century at the same time as the new buildings were being constructed against the interior of the fort wall. The south-east angle and latrine were probably rebuilt at this time *(56)*.
3   On the north rampart a narrow curtain wall was rebuilt in around AD 300 and a new rampart bank was constructed against the interior. There was evidence for further repairs before the part of the north curtain wall collapsed after the middle of the fourth century.

Using this basic framework for the chronology of the defences, it is possible to outline how the later Roman fort was defended.

*56* The south-west angle of the fort, showing the repairs carried out using long stone blocks. Similar work can be seen at the south-east angle and in other places on the outer face of the fort wall. *Hadrian's Wall Archive*

Firstly the gates; the narrowing and blocking of the west gate has already been discussed. No longer needed as an entrance, it was completely closed and access to the west and the Military Way was blocked by two banks and ditches *(colour plate 2)*. At Great Chesters fort, Housesteads' neighbour to the west, the blocking of the west gate survives and a late Roman ditch restricted entrance only to the south gate. The north gate and ditch is now obscured by farm buildings. At Housesteads only the south and east gates remained open, although both had been reduced to a single entrance or portal by this period. The north gate had been earlier restricted to a narrow postern and movement north of the Wall was channelled through the Knag Burn Gateway *(47)*.

Further evidence for these changes can be seen in the numbers of decorated string course blocks which are found reused in the curtain walls and as flagging and building stones in the new chalet-barracks of the fourth century. On the outer face of the fort wall and on Hadrian's Wall, there was a string course of chamfered stones marking the junction between the wall-top and parapet. These decorated blocks probably had a similar function but are likely to have come from the towers and fort gates, since a number are corner blocks from the external angles of towers. A large number of these stones survive, amounting to a total length of 65m (213ft). This is clearly too long for a single building so the towers and gates of the fort are obvious candidates. Their reuse implies that the towers were in a poor state of repair and were reconstructed from a low level, leaving the string course blocks available for use elsewhere *(57)*.

*57* The blocking wall on the east side of the north gate. Among the long stones used for blocking to the right can be seen a flat slab below the three square blocks. A broken socket is visible at the end of this stone. It can be identified as the upper slab in which the gates hung to either side of the central pier. There is a second socket at the far end of the slab, at the correct distance to allow it to rest on the blocks of the central pier. To remove this stone intact required the systematic demolition of the gate structure above. It is not certain when this occurred, but it indicates the way in which the structural grandeur of the gates was sacrificed to ensure the security of the fort. *Author*

Some idea of how radical some of these changes must have been can be seen at the north gate where the flat slab used as part of the mechanism to hang the gates, was built into the blocking of the later gate. To remove it intact required systematic demolition of the gate structure above. Further evidence for rebuilding of the gates can be seen at the east gate. The north gate-tower was rebuilt from its foundations and the external angle was reconstructed with ordinary wall stones, no longer supporting an arch over the gateway. In 1830 Hodgson had observed similar decay at the west gate, suggesting that the roof of the gallery across the gateway had collapsed before the gate was finally blocked.

The other major change in the defences was the reinstatement of the rampart bank behind the curtain. This is best known from the recent excavations at the north-east angle, but similar work was probably carried out elsewhere around the interior of the fort. A new retaining wall was constructed for the bank, including a reused pier base from the barracks. Contemporary with this work was the construction of two new interval towers added behind the curtain between the north and east gates. These were built with substantial foundations and were clearly intended to stand high above the curtain wall. Two other interval towers in the south-east angle belong to the same period of refortification. It is not known if there were additional towers on the west curtain of the fort.

It would appear therefore that at the same period that the new stores building XV was constructed and the barracks were being rebuilt, the defences of the fort underwent a major restoration. What is surprising about this new work is that the fort defences followed a pattern set two centuries before Hadrian's Wall was first built. By contrast the new fortifications of the Saxon Shore forts in southern Britain followed new designs in defensive architecture found throughout the Roman world, with projecting towers and thickened walls. On Hadrian's Wall no attempt was made to follow these new methods and there was a stubborn conservatism in the form of the defences. It is as if the builders at Housesteads and other forts on the Wall consciously rejected the newer, more ambitious forms, in favour of the established, traditional methods of fortification.

The evidence for the garrison for Hadrian's Wall in the fourth century, as it survives in the *Notitia Dignitatum,* presents a remarkable picture of the survival of units attested as part of the Wall garrison from inscriptions in the third century. Such continuity can only be paralleled on those frontiers whose armies remained relatively unscathed by the military disasters of the third and fourth centuries. Older theories about the withdrawal of regiments from the Wall garrison in the 290s to support the usurper Allectus, cannot be supported by the archaeological evidence. There are no clear signs of disruption and decay. Conversely it can be argued that the level of conservatism and apparent resistance to change, reflects military communities which had remained unaltered for several generations. However, the renovation of so much of the fort at Housesteads and elsewhere on the northern frontier implies some external stimulus from the military commanders in northern Britain or beyond.

## CONSTANTIUS I AND CONSTANTINE

It has already been seen that the Tetrarchic inscription from Birdoswald is the only securely dated record from any fort on the Wall at this period. There was a renewed level of imperial activity in Britain after AD 295 especially when the new Augustus, Constantius I, campaigned in the north with his son Constantine, against the Picts in AD 305. This was the first major imperial expedition north of the Wall since the campaigns of Septimius Severus and, as it happened, the last in the history of Roman Britain. Following Constantius' death in the following year, Constantine was acclaimed as Caesar at York and, throughout the northern frontier there are a remarkable series of inscribed milestones, including a group from Crindledykes on the Stanegate, dating to this period and later in Constantine's reign. It is not certain from the archaeological evidence how long these restorations at Housesteads took, although it would appear that the work was on a scale requiring activity over years rather than months. The fragmentary Tetrarchic inscription from Housesteads can be dated before AD 305 when Constantius became *Augustus.*

On Hadrian's Wall it is often possible to identify major building periods based on the archaeological and epigraphic evidence. It is more difficult however to integrate these 'construction episodes' with the very fragmentary historical texts. A continuous narrative of the history of the northern frontier is not feasible, but it is possible to recognise the effects of an imperial campaign in the archaeological record; it is as if the presence of the emperor had 'energised' the frontier province.


THE LATE ROMAN ARMY AT HOUSESTEADS

The Roman army of the late third and fourth centuries was different in many respects from the armies of Hadrian and Trajan. Following the crisis of the barbarian invasions and civil wars of the third century, a different military organisation had emerged by the reign of Constantine the Great (AD 306-32). The old division between the elite legions and the auxiliaries came to be of little significance and was replaced by the distinction between the frontier armies and the field armies. The field army (*comitatenses*) accompanied the emperor or senior army commanders and could be used to fight against invasion or internal opposition to imperial rule. The older frontier armies, such as that in northern Britain, and including the legions, were called the *limitanei* and were of lower status and pay than the field troops.[4]

Despite these changes in the status and organisation of the frontier garrisons, fourth-century emperors could not afford to ignore frontier defence. Historical sources frequently praise the achievements of emperors – indeed many of these works were not documents of record but works of propaganda. Some idea of a fourth century emperor's role in frontier defence can be gained from a contemporary orator, Themistius, who delivered a speech to the emperor Valens, in AD 370, praising in detail his restoration of the forts and garrisons of the lower Danube frontier: He [the emperor] built some completely new border forts, restored others that had fallen into disrepair and furnished others with what they required.' Among these requirements Themistius includes the telling phrase, 'soldiers from the lists and garrisons whose numbers were not fraudulent'. He complains further about the garrison commanders who 'reduced the numbers of those on guard duty so that the pay of those missing would fall to them. In this way the border forts fell into disrepair, denuded of men and arms. How far the garrisons on Hadrian's Wall were subject to such corrupt practices is unknown, although Themistius was not alone in remonstrating about such activities and, a number of later fourth century laws attempted to restrict the worst excesses of military commanders. Such factors need to be considered when attempting to interpret the structural evidence from a fort such as Housesteads.

In its overall plan the fort remained in the mould of its second-century predecessor – it was only different in the details of its appearance. Although 'a centurion of the old order might have blanched' at the state of some of the buildings, it remains unclear how much the internal organisation had significantly changed. The frontier army during the late third and fourth century throughout the empire evolved into a different organisation from its predecessors, but this came about less from deliberate reforms than the exigencies of local circumstances and the changing resources of the empire. Finds from the forts show clearly that the Wall zone remained a consumer of imported pottery and other materials. At the same time there is ample evidence to show that the soldiers received at least part of their pay in coinage.

After AD 320, much of the *vicus* seems to have been abandoned, but at the same time there is no direct proof that the families of soldiers constituted the majority of the *vicus* population. Indeed, the archaeological evidence would suggest that the 'chalets' were constructed several decades before. During the excavations of barrack XIII and the north-east ramparts in the late 1970s it was suggested that there were a significant number of artefacts normally associated with women or children and that the chalets were occupied by the families from the militia of soldier-farmers garrisoning the fort. Subsequent analysis has shown that these items were derived from the material introduced into the fort for the building of the new rampart bank, no doubt from the abandoned rubbish dumps of the *vicus*.

In conclusion, the change from a single barrack to chalet-barracks probably did not significantly effect the number of soldiers that could be accommodated in the fort, since in the third century the number of *contubernia* had already been reduced by one in barrack XIV. The total strength of the garrison probably did fall during the relatively peaceful decades of the third century, possibly due to corrupt practice described by late Roman writers. At the same time there is little to support the view that there was a massive reduction of the effective strength and that part of the accommodation was replaced by the soldiers' families and other non-combatants. Certainly some parts of the fort, like the hospital and much of the granary, were occupied by domestic occupation, but there is no way of determining if it was civil or military in character and the date of these changes remains uncertain.

The uniform construction of the chalet-barracks, together with the new stores building and the major repairs carried out in the central range, can all be interpreted to demonstrate a continuing, vigorous military presence at Housesteads in the first decades of the fourth century.

## THE LATER FOURTH CENTURY

Despite extensive rebuilding of the curtain wall, the defences underwent continuing alterations and repair, best known from the excavations at the north-east corner[5] *(58)*. The rampart bank behind the north curtain was repeatedly rebuilt with new retaining walls. It was increasingly widened to the east, so that eventually the *intervallum* road became no more than an alley 1.5m (5ft) wide. The only explanation for such excessive repairs is that the curtain wall had partly collapsed and was replaced by a wider bank. At some time after the middle of the fourth century, the stone interval tower was replaced with a timber structure, with great timber post-holes cut into the inside angles of the tower. The fort was still

*58* The north rampart to the north of barrack XIII during excavations in 1978, from the south-east. The photograph shows the sequence of retaining walls built for the rampart. The stone platform to the right of the photograph is the foundations of the late interval tower, constructed as part of the increased defences of the fort during the fourth century. *Author*

defended but it came to resemble more closely the defences of an Iron Age hillfort than the regular fortifications of the Roman imperial army. Similar defences with an earth rampart and a narrow stone parapet have been also found at Birdoswald. The two of the southern angle towers were rebuilt at this time. At the south-east angle the tower was constructed with a separate external wall. Similar modifications can be seen at the south-west angle. Both towers now stood independent of the curved exterior angle of the curtain, which could have been rebuilt as a rampart bank.

At the east gate some of the rebuilding has already been described, but perhaps the most impressive feature of the latest period of the Roman defences is a slot cut into the stonework of the outer face of the central pier. This supported a timber upright, possibly reused from one of the main building such as the east end of the storehouse, and used to carry a wooden lintel across the gate. The chalet-barracks demonstrate continued modifications and changes, parts were demolished and buildings began to encroach onto the streets. The very latest, possibly post-Roman occupation was observed in the west and east ends of XIII in the form of small circular or sub-circular structures, constructed within or partly over the existing chalet walls. At the east end of the street between buildings XIII and XIV, a layer of dark soil containing late Roman pottery was sealed by layers of flagging arranged in a distinctive keel shape and representing the fragmentary remains of buildings of late or sub-Roman date.

## BATHS IN BUILDING XV

The most important new building that survives within the fort from this period was the construction of a small bath house at the east end of building XV *(colour plate 17)*. The east end of the storehouse was demolished and a new east end wall was built. The baths were excavated by Hodgson in 1831, who describes them as follows:

> Some of the stones of the pillars of the stove had elegant mouldings upon them, and had plainly been used in former buildings. It consisted of two apartments, divided by a party wall of two feet. The first, or ante-room, which was supported by six pillars, was 11½ft by 8ft, and floored in the ordinary way by freestone flags, covered by a composition of lime and pounded tiles. The second was 7ft square within, and wholly covered floor and sides, with a similar cement 6in thick, the last coating being finer than the rest and finely polished. On its north side, immediately under the mouth of the flue, were thin stones set on edge between the outward wall and the plaster: and on the west side, two upright rows of tufaceous limestone, porous as pumice stone, one 6in, the other 5in broad, were inserted in the wall, apparently for allowing heat to rise from below without the smoke. As the mouth of the stove was over this division of the building, it would have more advantage of the fire than the ante-room, especially as the opening for the smoke seemed to be behind a wall of pillars at the north-east corner of the building, and quite near the mouth of the mouth of the furnace. Adjoining to the entrance in to the ante-room was a large and perfect cistern, apparently for cold water, and formed on the inside of the usual Roman composition of pounded tile and lime, and probably having in it a portion of pounded limestone.

This is of the earliest and one of the most detailed accounts of the excavation of any of the buildings in the fort. The baths were L-shaped with an entrance from the *via praetoria* into a cold room with a small cold bath. Traces of the pink water-proof mortar still survive. From here the bather entered a warm room, followed by a hot bath. The raised floors which Hodgson described have now decayed and only a few of the pillars survive. The hot bath may have been situated in the east alcove. On one of its upper south quoins there is a carved phallus, looking like a pair of spectacles. Hodgson observed the tufa blocks used in the walls, although such blocks were also used in the vaulting of baths. The space behind the furnace remained open and was at a much lower level than the floor of the main building to the west, so that it became necessary to cut a drainage channel through the east foundation of the storehouse, the blocks above must have been already removed.

The problems of water supply have already been discussed and no permanent source was available inside the fort. It was for this reason that the Hadrianic bath house was placed 250m (760ft) to the east across the valley of the Knag Burn.

These fourth-century baths are altogether smaller and must have gathered water from within the fort, perhaps from the wide roof of the storehouse immediately to the west. In fact the water requirements of a small baths such as these were limited, and the water was changed much less regularly than modern sanitary requirements might expect. Little is known about the building history of the Knag Burn baths, but the use of tufa blocks, which are found nowhere else in the fort, could suggest that the special building stones were taken for use in the smaller baths when these replaced the more distant, earlier baths in the valley.

The implication of this new bath house was a reduced demand for communal bathing, perhaps indicating that the garrison was smaller, or alternatively a change of habit, a lessening of Romanised ways. Equally significant is the move inside the fort which could mean that there was a greater concern for security, already shown by the rebuilding and repairs to the defences.

# 9

# AFTER THE ROMANS

Exactly how the Roman occupation of Housesteads ended is not known, although it is certain it did not finish in the orgy of destruction sometimes depicted in popular accounts. What signifies the end most clearly to the archaeologist is the breakdown of the supply system of coins, metalwork and pottery which had continued to reach the garrisons on the Wall throughout the fourth century. The latest coins known from Hadrian's Wall date within a year or so of the latest coins from the province as a whole, showing that there was no immediate rundown of the garrisons on the Wall before the western emperor, Honorius, declared the cities of Britain to be self-reliant for their defence.

The garrison on Hadrian's Wall was an artificial creation, maintained by the resources and expenditure of the Roman state and this is nowhere more apparent than at Housesteads. Whatever the resources of the locality, it could not alone support the garrison, even a reduced late Roman regiment, without external support. The continued maintenance of the storehouse XV in the fort throughout the fourth century shows how this system of provision for the Wall garrisons continued. Since the end of Roman rule, the population at Housesteads is unlikely ever to have exceeded 20-30 persons, which gives some idea of the population level the neighbourhood could naturally sustain; the Roman level was far in excess of this figure.

Once imperial authority and payments were severed in AD 407, the garrison and their dependants left, rather like an old mining town after the gold rush. There is no specific evidence for the occupation of the fort after the Romans; the recent claim that the fort was held and re-defended in the Dark Ages is based on the mistaken identification of a spearhead as Anglo-Saxon, but it is a type well attested amongst Roman finds. The absence of post-Roman material is in contrast with many other forts. An early Christian gravestone of a man called *Brigomaglos* was found at Vindolanda and there are other Anglo-Saxon artefacts from that site.[1] Overlooking Vindolanda is the earlier hillfort of Barcombe, whose modern name could preserve elements of *Vercovicium*, the Roman name for Housesteads. The more sheltered situation of Vindolanda gave access to the fertile farmland of the valley of the South Tyne and it is possible that the two communities combined in the uncertain times of the fifth and sixth centuries. The reoccupation of earlier hilltop defences is not uncommon at this period and, the old hill-fort of Barcombe could have became a focus for the descendants of the garrison, who adopted the district name of Housesteads – *Vercovicium*.

A local parallel for the continuity of Roman place names and their usage to denote a district rather than a place exists at the nearby fort of Great Chesters. The Roman name, *Aesica*, appears to have survived into the late seventh century when a life of St Cuthbert recounted a miracle at *Ahse*. The Saint was travelling from Hexham towards Carlisle and halted about midway at a place the Latin text refers to as a *mansio*, although this need not be understood literally in its Roman sense as meaning an inn or road station. Cuthbert appears to have been following either the Stanegate or the Military Way, roads which were to remain as important routes until the eighteenth century. The Saint's life recounts how people 'gathered together from the mountains' at Ahse to see the Saint who blessed and preached to them and miraculously cured a boy. *Ahse* is described as a district, not a place and, if the identification with *Aesica* is accepted, it demonstrates how Roman names could persist, even when the settlements themselves had withered away.

A POSSIBLE CHURCH AT HOUSESTEADS?

Despite the absence of specific artefacts from Housesteads which can be dated to the fifth or sixth centuries, there is tantalizing structural evidence for Christianity within the fort dating from either the late-Roman or immediate post-Roman periods. Bosanquet's excavations in the north part of the fort revealed part of a stone building between barrack I and building VII. He described it in 1898 as having, 'a rude pavement of massive building stones and flags roughly fitted together', separated from the surface of the *intervallum* road by a layer of dark soil *(59 and 5)*. The walls of the building survived best at the west end where 'they rested directly on the pavement' and were curved, forming part of an apse. The full curve of this apse did not survive but was reconstructed in Bosanquet's plan of the site. It appears to be a small chapel-like structure, 6m (20ft) wide and at least 10m (33ft) long, constructed on soil which had accumulated after the abandonment of buildings I and VII.

In 1898 the curtain to the north of this building was not fully exposed, but later clearance revealed the remains of an early interval tower lying to the north of the apsidal building with a stone flagged water tank to the south-west of it. There is no record of when this excavation was undertaken, but surviving inside the water tank are the remains of a stone cist aligned from east to west. This comprises a number of slabs, mostly reused Roman stones, set on edge to define a long rectangle against the north side of the tank *(60)*. The cist is clearly later in date than the tank and the remainder of the interior of the tank was intentionally paved with large slabs. Stone cists were used in burials from the Bronze Age to the

*59* View from the south-east of Bosanquet's excavation of the apsidal structure close to the north rampart, possibly a church; compare with figure 5. *Hadrian's Wall Archive, 1898*

eighteenth century, but they are especially found in northern Britain and Ireland in the early Christian period, from the fourth to eighth centuries AD. Many of these, but not necessarily all, can be shown to be Christian burials and are often aligned east to west. One cist burial enclosing a wooden coffin was set north-south and was found in a *vicus* building, east of the spring and shrine below Chapel Hill. Two other cists are known beside Hadrian's Wall. One was uncovered in the course of consolidation to the east of Sewingshields milecastle. It was aligned with the Wall, and was east-west in orientation. Another was found east of Birdoswald Fort in a similar position; no trace now remains apart from an archive photograph. Both are clearly later than the Wall but are probably Roman in origin although there is no other indication of date or associated finds *(61)*.

At Housesteads there can be no doubt, however, that the water tank was reused as a grave of this type most commonly found in the Scottish Borders and the Celtic West. The proximity of the long cist to the apse-ended structure is intriguing and raises the question whether the two are connected. While the purpose of the building on its own cannot not be readily identified, the close association with the distinctive east-west oriented grave can be interpreted as a church. Taken together, the long cist and the apse-ended building offer some of the most intriguing evidence for Christianity to survive from Hadrian's Wall.

The identification of buildings as churches in Britain in the fourth and fifth centuries remains controversial but a number of churches have been recognised in Britain and elsewhere in the Western Roman Empire, orientated towards the west

60 The water tank located south of the north interval tower, as seen from the east. The edge-stones for the later burial define a cist to the right of the tank. *Hadrian's Wall Archive*

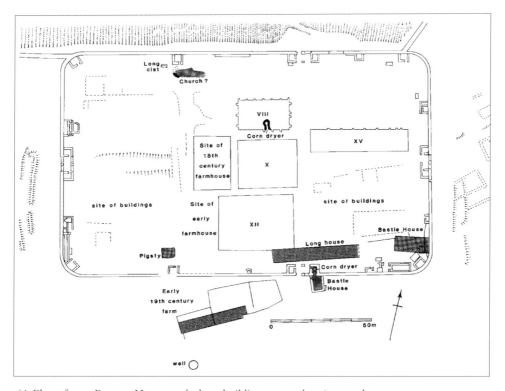

61 Plan of post-Roman Housesteads; later buildings up to the nineteenth century

rather than to the east, which later became normal practice. Excavations at Vindolanda in 1998 within the commanding officers house revealed the unexpected remains of a similar apse-ended building located in the middle of the courtyard. Its location suggests that the building either belonged to the very final Roman or sub-Roman phases at the fort. In size it is very similar to the Housesteads structure, almost exactly the same width of 6m and a length of at least 9m, although there are difference in construction and how the two buildings have survived. The identification of the structure at Vindolanda as a church can be supported by other evidence from the site, notably the well-known fifth-century tombstone of Brigomaglus and other early Christian objects known from recent excavations, although there are no known late burials from within the fort. At Housesteads the location of the cist within the fort strongly suggests that the burial occurred after the main period of occupation, since normal Roman funerary practice insisted on burials outside of settlements. Without further archaeological evidence it remains possible that the 'chapel' was the church for the garrison at the end of the fourth century, which later survived as the religious focus for part of the district, thus explaining the later burial.

The only example from Britain of a late Roman church functioning within a fort has been recognised at Richborough on the coast of Kent. However, many later Saxon and medieval churches lie within the area of earlier forts, such as Lanchester in County Durham and Bewcastle to the north of Hadrian's Wall. Bewcastle serves as an instructive parallel to Housesteads. The fort there was abandoned like many of the outposts north of the Wall in the early fourth century, yet in the seventh century within the circuit of the earlier fort was erected a magnificent carved stone cross, one of the masterpieces of Northumbrian art. At Bewcastle in the immediate centuries after the end of Roman rule, there was clearly some continuity of 'place', as a focus for the religious and probably also the economic and political life of the area. It is possible to imagine that *Ahse*, Great Chesters, functioned in a similar way, as described in the account of St Cuthbert's visit. The possible church and the long cist at Housesteads show that the site of the fort also retained local significance in the centuries after AD 407, but that it failed to develop as a local or regional Christian centre like other former forts such as Bewcastle. In addition to those later Christian sites further evidence has recently been collected relating to similar buildings from a number of places in the northern England and Scotland. These are mostly very similar in size to the examples from Housesteads and Vindolanda, and have been described as D-ended buildings associated with Roman-period settlements, including the major native hillfort and tribal centre at Traprain Law in south-east Scotland.[2]

Today many of the rural churches in Cumbria and Northumberland appear to have been situated in remote, often lonely places, but their location can mask an earlier, often ancient, role as the focus for dispersed communities, route centres and drove roads. For much of the Middle Ages, Housesteads lay beyond the main areas of rural settlement and it is significant that the closest medieval church lies on the south side of the Tyne at Beltingham, a place-name indicating an early Anglo-Saxon settlement, no longer reliant on Roman origins.

## SETTLEMENT AND LAND USE

Hadrian's Wall in the central sector occupies a zone of transition between the settled arable land of the Tyne Valley and the high mosses and moors which extend north towards the Scottish border, now largely afforested by the Kielder and Wark forests. The Whin Sill, and hence the Wall, goes a long way to define the limit of permanent settlement but the exact position of this northern edge fluctuates throughout history on either side of this line. There is no written record of Housesteads in the medieval period; the closest documented places are Sewingshields Castle to the east and Bradley Hall to the south-west. The fort and much of Hadrian's Wall as far west as Walltown, was on the margin of the waste known since the twelfth century as the Huntlands, or from the number of small lakes or 'loughs', as the Forest of Lowes. This name first appears in 1326, and as late as 1586 the area was described as 'one great waste and uncultivated parcel of ground called the forest of Lowes'.

The end of Roman rule in the north appears to have had a significant effect on the landscape and vegetation of the uplands. Recent studies of the pollen cores from a number of mires in the frontier zone have suggested that, although there had been extensive forest clearance during the Roman period, from the late fourth century onwards there was a phase of re-forestation which continued into the Middle Ages. What is surprising is that this change was localised to the northern military zone and nowhere else in the former Roman province of Britain was there significant re-forestation. It can be argued that the Roman army had made intensive and specific demands on the landscape; once the garrisons were removed less intensive land-use continued until the seventeenth century.

The closest medieval settlement to Housesteads was at Bradley Hall and the earliest reference seems to occur in the thirteenth century. In 1306 the hall and settlement were substantial enough to offer accommodation to Edward I and his retinue on 5 and 6 September as he progressed across England towards Carlisle, in part at least following the Stanegate or Karelgate (Carlisle Street), as it was known in the Middle Ages. From Tynedale Edward moved on to Lanercost Priory, where he passed the winter before assembling his army at Burgh-by-Sands for an invasion of Scotland that was curtailed by the king's death. The remains of little more than a bastle house survive within the modern farm, the hall does not figure in the 1415 list of Border Strongholds, and it was found to be 'lying waste and unplenished' in 1541.

If little survives of Edward I's hall at Bradley, around the farm and to the east of the burn are the remains of medieval fields and a hamlet *(62)*, the traces of a settlement on the margin that never quite succeeded as a village. The house

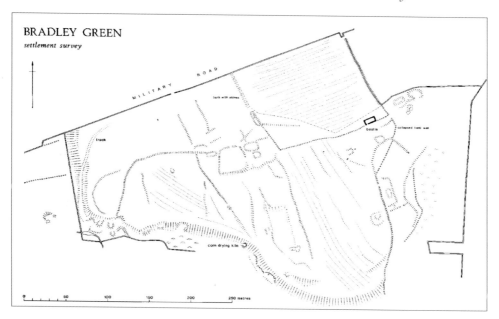

**BRADLEY GREEN**
*settlement survey*

62 Survey of the medieval and early modern settlement at Bradley Green. Bradley Hall, where Edward I is recorded to have stayed, lies on the west side of the Bradley Burn. *Drawn by Brian Williams; the National Trust*

platforms are aligned with a large bank apparently dividing the cultivated land to the south from the waste to the north. Sixteenth-century documents record this settlement as Easter Bradley and the house platforms were followed by more substantial stone-built bastles in the late sixteenth century.[3]

Another medieval structure along the Wall is unrecorded in the documentary sources; this is the Peel Tower which gives its name to Peel Crags and other places around. It comprises a tower or stone farmhouse constructed across the partly demolished line of Hadrian's Wall. Pottery from the tower can be dated to the fourteenth century. It does not occupy the more prominent and defensible position at Steel Rigg, and it was probably no more than a medieval farmstead associated with the drove road that today runs down the hill past the Youth Hostel at Twice Brewed and on to the village of Henshaw. Pottery of a similar date has been found in the excavations of other medieval buildings constructed on the line of the Wall, identified as 'shielings'. These are first mentioned in medieval documents concerned with the Huntlands from as early as the late twelfth century and are the key for understanding how much of the uplands were used at this period.

A shieling or shiel was defined by a seventeenth-century visitor to North-umberland as 'a cottage made in open places of turf and flag'. The name survives in place names common along the Wall, such as Winshields and High Shield and many more, although it is not confined to the uplands, as witnessed by South

Shields, the site of fisherman's shiels or huts at the mouth of the Tyne. One of the best-known accounts of shielings was by William Camden, who visited parts of Hadrian's Wall in 1599. He presents an eye-witness description of the district of Gilsland in north-east Cumbria:

> Here every way round about in the wasts as they terme them, as also in Giliesland, you mey see as it were the ancient Nomades, a martiall kinde of men, who from the moneth of Aprill unto August, lye out scattering and summering (as they tearme it) with their cattell in little cottages here and there which they call Sheales and Shealings.

Camden described a form of seasonal management of the upland resource found throughout highland Britain and Ireland. It is properly termed transhumance by geographers and today is more familiar in the Mediterranean parts of Europe. In the Lake District the local word for these pastures is scales but in Northumberland they were known as shieling or shielding grounds, both words being Norse in origin. In the north of Northumberland it was the custom in the sixteenth century to gather on the upland pastures according to surname, rather like Scottish clans, but this practice is not recorded in Tynedale where the shielings were directly linked with the villages in the valley. Modern parish boundaries remain little changed between Haydon Bridge and Haltwhistle and they all display similar features. Each parish cuts a long narrow transect across the full range of agricultural resources: from the meadows and arable of the valley, to the permanent and seasonal pasture of the uplands and the waste. This continues the same pattern as the medieval villages in the Tyne valley except that there were fewer outlying farmsteads. Housesteads and the Roman Wall were parcelled out between the villages in the valley, and the Wall was a ready quarry for the construction of these medieval summer homes.[4]

Shielings are often found in groups and the most detailed study has been carried out on those around the isolated hill, *Mons Fabricius*, to the east of Castle Nick *(63)*. A row of four shielings was built on the level hilltop, nestled into the collapse of the Wall. They were small rectangular houses built with dry-stone walls, measuring 8.5m long by 2.5m (28ft x 8ft) wide, each had been repaired and rebuilt a number of times. The earliest pottery dated to the fourteenth century, but later flagged floors and hearths could be dated to the early sixteenth century. A distinct trackway led up to the shielings around the side of the hill. Another scattered group of seven shielings was clustered around the lower slopes of the hill and over the ruins of milecastle 39. Unlike the upper row, which was constructed of stones from the Roman Wall, most of these used the unhewn whinstone boulders from the hillside. They were similar in area to the upper group but in part, at least, were constructed of turf. There were very few finds from the four that were excavated and it is difficult to say how many of these buildings were occupied simultaneously. For instance it is not clear whether the upper group is

*63* Reconstruction of shielings on Mons Fabricius. These are known to date from the fourteenth to the sixteenth century. Others at the base of the crag could be earlier in date. *After R. Mills: the National Trust*

contemporary with the lower group. Those constructed against the Wall had the advantage of better observation and some protection, while those around the base of the hill were more sheltered from the prevailing weather.

Sewingshields, to the east of Housesteads and at the eastern extremity of the crags, presents a complex pattern of medieval settlement. Here the picture is enriched not just by a castle but also by King Arthur. The antiquity of this Arthurian legend at Sewingshields is not known. Hodgson dismissed legends about the castle and it was left to Collingwood Bruce to recount how a lone shepherd lost his knitting while minding his flock and chanced upon King Arthur and his knights asleep in a cavern below Sewingshields Crags. This need be no more than a local folk tale, which has nothing to contribute to the already bulky literature on Arthur and Dark Age archaeology.

North of the crags and on an old route leading from the South Tyne valley towards Wark and the North Tyne, Sewingshields Castle survives in the traces of a stone tower, fish ponds and possibly a moated site, all characteristic of a manor of at least thirteenth-century date, and it is thought that the earliest permanent settlement dates from the eleventh century. The place name of Sewingshields indicates that the settlement was preceded by a shieling belonging to 'Sigewine'. By the fifteenth century the manor was in decline and, like Bradley Hall, it was described in 1541 as ruinous and the ground about it was used only 'to pasture in summer time'. There is a clear pattern to the history of land use at Sewingshields. In the tenth and eleventh centuries this was a shieling ground, later forming part of a permanent manor, which by the fifteenth and sixteenth centuries had returned to only seasonal use.

Excavations on the site of Sewingshields milecastle (35) found the remains of a small medieval settlement lying over the Roman buildings which have been described as a group of shielings. In fact, the medieval structures are more complex than either the contemporary descriptions of shielings or other excavated examples would suggest. A further factor is the relative wealth of the finds from this settlement which are inappropriate for mere herdsmen. These include a decorated spur and a variety of glazed pottery, all of which are more characteristic of a castle or the dwelling of higher status individuals, perhaps in this case used as a hunting lodge. An alternative explanation is that these 'treasures' were robbers' loot close to the notorious haunt at Busy Gap less than 1km (half a mile) to the west.

How can these patterns of land use which are repeated elsewhere in the marginal uplands in northern England be explained? One possibility is the fluctuations in pattern of the Earth's climate. Between AD 700 and 1300 there was a warm episode in the climate called the Little Optimum; this period was followed by the Little Ice Age, lasting to 1850. It is possible to explain the permanent settlement of marginal areas seen at Bradley Hall, Peel Tower and Sewingshields as determined by these climatic changes, but other factors also need to be considered. One is demographic; as a consequence of the Little Optimum the population of Britain increased throughout the twelfth and thirteenth centuries, creating greater pressure for arable land. There was an expansion of settlement up to marginal lands seen on Dartmoor, the Yorkshire Dales and here represented by the settlements like Sewingshields, Bradely Hall and possibly Housesteads adjacent to the Wall. After the expansion in to the uplands, the fourteenth century brought a series of devastating crises. Between 1315 and 1318 there were catastrophic harvests and the uplands were especially vulnerable, partly because the ecologically marginal land was prone to exhaustion as well as being liable to climatic deterioration and crop failure. The pattern throughout the British Isles was of a weakened population which then succumbed to the Black Death, in 1348 and later years. Within two generations the country's population had fallen disastrously and, in 1500, when there is evidence for the occupation of the shielings near Castle Nick, England was hardly more populous than at the time of the Domesday Book 450 years before.

At Housesteads itself there is no direct archaeological or historical evidence for settlement contemporary with Sewingshields Castle or Bradley Hall. Recalling, however, the unexpected discovery of a medieval tower-house at Peel Gap, it is unlikely that the fertile fields south of the fort were untended during the period of greatest population expansion in the thirteenth and early fourteenth centuries. Certainly renewed arable farming at this period could help to explain the great variety of fields which now survive around the fort. It is also possible that the long-house behind the south gate was first occupied at this period. Some shielings are also known: a pair lie just north of the Wall east of the valley of the Knag Burn and the excavation of barrack XIV records a late building of similar size over the Roman structures. These are likely to date after the fourteenth century crisis and 'the retreat from the margin'.

## HOUSESTEADS ON A TUDOR FRONTIER

The name of 'House steads' is first recorded in the sixteenth century when it was owned by Nicholas Crane of Bradley Hall,[5] but the site also appears under the name of 'Chesters in the Wall near Busygap'. The earliest reference to the area occurs a few years before in the schedule of the Border Watch set out in the Border Survey of 1542. Starting at the Tipalt Burn in the west, it lists the positions of the watches to guard against infiltration from the north. It stated that two watchmen were to be stationed between Caw Gap and Knagburn Head. Knagburn Head must be the valley of the Knag Burn immediately to the east of Housesteads and the watch probably corresponds to one on the Bradley Beacons reported in 1550. It is significant that the permanent settlement itself is not yet mentioned at this date. Later in the sixteenth century the land was divided among a number of tenants. Hugh Crawhawe (Crowhall) in 1568 held lands in Crawhawe, Hawesteads, Crindledykes and Bradley Hall, as well as other places in Thorngrafton. Nicholas Crane of Crowhall settled on his daughter as part of a marriage settlement in 1615 similar properties at Crawhall, Bradley Hall, Easter Bradley, Housesteads and Cringledykes and other places again in the parish of Thorngrafton.

These bare records of ownership scarcely hint at the notoriety of the district in Tudor and Stuart times. Hodgson wrote in 1840: 'All the wild country along each side of the Roman Wall from Walltown to Walwick had been immemorially celebrated as the fastness of gangs of thieves, till their sanctuary of cruelty and rapine was finally invaded by the Military Road that made through it in the middle of the last century.' The first antiquaries to make a serious study of the Roman remains in the north, Camden and Cotton, visited the Wall in 1599 *(64)* and Camden wrote of the Wall: 'Verily I have seen the tract of it over the high pitches and steep descent of hills, wonderfully rising and falling.' Yet for much of the central sector they dared not go along the Wall to places he called Chester-in-the-Wall, Busy Gap, Iverton and Forsten. Of these the first is thought to be Housesteads, Busy Gap is known to the east of the fort, but the other two cannot be definitely identified. Camden wrote: 'I could not safely take the full survey of it for fear of the rank robbers thereabouts.'

The rank robbers, Busy Gap rogues and moss-troopers were all representatives of a border society which had grown up over three centuries of conflict between the kingdoms of England and Scotland. Housesteads lay in the Middle March, one of three frontier commands along the border and, until 1495 it was in the lordship of Tynedale and independent of the rest of Northumberland. Scotland had not always been the natural enemy and from 1158 to 1296 the Lordship was held by the kings of Scotland and the border did not take its current line until the middle of the fourteenth century. Even after Edward I's invasions, Bradley Hall was still called 'on the Scottish marches'. The thirteenth and fourteenth century witnessed major invasions and reprisals between the two nations, but it can be questioned

WILLIAM CAMBDEN Clarenciaux king of
Armes. He dyed at Westminster Anno Dm̄ 1 6 2 3
Aged 7 4 yeares

*64* William Camden, a Tudor antiquary and author of *Britannia*. He visited the Roman Wall in 1599 but was unable to visit the central sector of the Wall because of moss-troopers and Busy Gap rogues. *Hadrian's Wall Archive*

how far this effected the isolated farmsteads and shieling grounds of the central sector. In the fifteenth and sixteenth centuries however, there was a change in the pattern of the conflict. Although it was orchestrated by the powers in London and Edinburgh, it was expressed in small scale raiding and skirmishes, across the border but also amongst the Border families and, increasingly a distinct border society evolved, with its own loyalties and enmities. In 1542 a report on the state of the Border defences recommended the defence of the castles at Sewingshields and Carraw to prevent 'the dread incursions of thieves... either coming from out of Liddesdale or from Tynedale lying both north of the said fortresses or else from out of Gilsland and Bewcastle lying also westward from the said houses'. A few years before, a raiding party of men from Liddesdale had rested at Busy Gap before descending on Haydon Bridge to steal cattle. It is apparent that the problem was not with the Scots alone and a level of lawlessness pervaded the Border country. This state of affairs continued long after the accession of James I in 1603, even if a Jacobean poet might claim:

> No wall of Hadrian serves to separate
> Our mutual love, nor our obedience:
> Being subject all to one Imperial Prince.

The borders were scarcely safe at the end of Charles II's reign, when they were visited by the Lord Chancellor, Francis North. Even by the standards of the age the Border country was noted for its rough justice. Suspicion was held by the Border keepers as good as proof and the inevitable sentence was the gallows. The Lord Chancellor travelled across to Carlisle, having been armed by the Sheriff of Northumberland for the journey. The account of his travels provides a vivid picture of a world which had changed little since the *Brittunculi* of the first century AD. On the road to Hexham:

> His lordship saw the true image of a Border country. The tenants of the several manors are bound to guard the judges through their precinct; and out of it they would not go not an inch, to save the souls of them. They were a comical sort of people, riding upon negs, as they called their small horses, with long beards, cloaks, and long broad swords, with basket hilts, hanging in broad belts that their legs and swords almost touched the ground; and every one in his turn, with his short cloak, and other equipage, came up cheek by jowl, and talked with my lord judge. His lordship was very pleased with their discourse; for they were great antiquarians in their own grounds.

Throughout the seventeenth century Housesteads continued to be a haunt of thieves and was owned by the infamous Armstrongs of Gandy's Knowe, and is today a ruined farmstead above the modern road to Vindolanda. The main structural remains from this period are the bastle house by the south gate and the long house within it *(colour plate 14)*. A bastle house is the name given to a specific type of stone-built house common in the Borders throughout the sixteenth and seventeenth centuries, a type described in the account of the Francis North's visit. It relates that:

> The Border trade [cattle thieving] was so great a mischief that all the considerable farmhouses (the houses of gentlemen were castles of course) were built of stone in the manner of a square tower, with an overhanging battlement, and, underneath the cattle were lodged every night. In the upper room the family lodged, and, when the alarm came, they went up to the top, and, with hot water and stones from the battlements, fought in defence of their cattle.

Not all were substantial enough to have upper battlements, but the division between a lower room for cattle and an upper living room without direct access between the two, is the basic definition of the bastle house. The example against the outside of the south gate at Housesteads is smaller than many of the better documented groups of bastles known in Redesdale and North Tynedale. The ground floor entrance lies midway along the side wall – a feature it shares with the bastles found at Bradley Green and at Gandy's Knowe nearby. The ground-floor doorway is on the west side and the door mouldings are quite distinct from

*65* An early photograph showing the south gate and the entrance to the bastle house on the east side. *Hadrian's Wall Archive*

Roman work *(65)*. The ground floor has a number of narrow loop windows, including one cut through the masonry of the north wall of the guard chamber, which formed a second room on the ground floor. In the narrow loop south of the doorway is part of a Roman window head, used as the bottom sill. The upper floor was entered from the east side, where steps gave access across the outer wall and a separate, probably later, set of steps are located near the south-east corner.

Bastles rarely occur singly and a second is known from nineteenth-century descriptions to have been located a little north of the south-east angle tower. Within the south gate was a different building, a long-house over 43m (141ft) in length, part of which was cleared away in the 1930s to allow better access in to the interior of the fort. The reused Roman stonework is less carefully selected and arranged than in the bastle walls, which might suggest an earlier date. The building has suffered at the hands of Roman archaeologists and we cannot now be sure how it fits into the pattern of later farms within the fort. Its position straddling the south entrance suggests that it is quite possibly the first settlement, dating to the middle ages which was then reinstated in the sixteenth and seventeenth centuries and formed part of a group of dwellings at that time. Later the bastle at the south gate is known to have gone out of use by the time a corn-drying kiln was placed in the guard chamber of the gate. This may be connected with the later occupation of the long-house, since another corn-drying kiln known from the granary

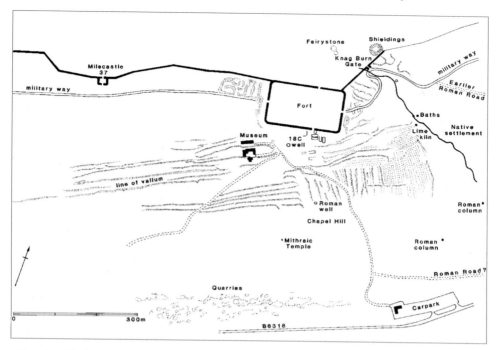

66 A simplified plan showing traces of the Roman, and later medieval, landscape around Housesteads. *Based on a survey by RCHME*

can be associated with the farmhouse shown in Stukeley's illustration of the site. Corn-drying kilns are a common feature of upland farms in the seventeenth and eighteenth centuries and at Housesteads attest the extent of arable farming at this period *(66)*.

In the early seventeenth century the land around the fort was subdivided between a number of tenants and was described by one Nick Gibson in 1629 as 'intermixing dale by dale with a tenement', a reference to a number of landhold-ings held by Gibsons, Nixons and later Armstrongs. Many of these men were notorious thieves. In 1604 one resident of Housesteads, Hugh Nixon, is recorded as a stealer of cattle and a receiver of stolen goods in the Lord Howard's Household Books for the Dacre Estates at Gilsland. Most notorious were the Armstrongs who gave the site a fearsome criminal reputation. The family only came into Tynedale late in the seventeenth century, spilling across the Scottish border when their lair in Liddesdale was finally suppressed. They are recorded as tenants and briefly as freeholders at Housesteads from 1663 onwards when they operated a ring of horse-thieves, ranging as far north as Perth and south as far as the Midlands. Nicholas Armstrong was eventually hanged for his crimes in 1704, while his brothers sought their fortune in America.

Evidently there was not enough income from horse-rustling, since surviving records show that the Armstrongs were mortgaged up to the hilt from 1688

*67* The Reverend John Hodgson. He was the earliest scholar of the Roman Wall to show convincingly that it was built by Hadrian. In his notebooks he was the first to record systematically, and in detail, much of the structure of the Wall and forts in the central sector. *Hadrian's Wall Archive*

onwards. Although Nicholas was able to purchase the freehold in 1692, his brothers sold their holdings two years later. He finally gave up the struggle in 1698 when both tenements were purchased by Thomas Gibson of Hexham six years before the law caught up with him. Hodgson *(67)*, in his *History of Northumberland*, records that a very low price of £58 was paid by Gibson for the farm, but this figure seems to be in error and the seventeenth-century title deeds preserved among John Clayton's papers record a much higher sum of £485, reflecting the good soil around the fort and at least the potential of some cereal production.[6] But far more than improving just the agricultural possibilities of the fort, the departure of the Armstrongs and the end of their border, opened up the site to visitors. After 1,300 years of Dark Ages, Housesteads once more emerged as a centre of more than just local significance.

# 10

# 'THE GRANDEST STATION
# IN THE WHOLE LINE'

Within four years of Gibson's purchase of the site, the earliest antiquarian account of a visit was published by Christopher Hunter, despite the continuing tenancy of the Armstrongs until 1704. He was to be the first of a steady stream of visitors over the next thirty years, encouraged by the new edition of Camden's *Britannia* in 1695. The fort was first represented on Warburton's *Map of Northumberland* (1716) and shown to lie immediately south of the 'Mountainous and Desert Uninhabited Grounds of the Forest of Lowes'. Most early visitors were concerned with the inscriptions and sculptures, but in 1724, Alexander Gordon, who explored the site with Sir John Clerk, 'caused the place to be dug where we were then sitting amidst the ruinous streets of this famous oppidum'. Stukeley arrived with Roger Gale in the following year and wrote that the remains were 'as ruined but yesterday'. His rough sketch is the earliest illustration of the site and shows a single farmhouse built over the hospital *(1)*.

Stukeley's account was not published for another 50 years and Horsley (who visited before 1730) provides the earliest methodical description of the inscriptions and remains in *Britannia Romana*. This is notable also for a good location map and an inset plan, showing the correct relationship of the fort to the Wall, a feature not repeated until MacClaughlan's survey of 1852-54.

At the beginning of the nineteenth century the site continued to inspire great admiration. William Hutton (see Chapter 1) described it as 'the Grandest Station in the whole line', and estimated the combined area of the fort and *vicus* at 15 acres (6 hectares). In the same year the Revd John Skinner similarly reckoned it to be the most interesting site on his journey along the Wall. Lingard echoed these sentiments in 1807: 'A most wonderful station. It abounds with remains.' He was also the first to observe the vertical offsets in the south face of Hadrian's Wall.

Throughout the eighteenth century Housesteads was farmed by a single tenant farmer and the extension of the area under plough, in and around the fort, resulted in the steady trawl of new antiquities to feed the visiting antiquarians' appetites. The Gibsons showed little concern for the Roman buildings which were plundered for field walls and other uses. At the time of the discovery of the Mithraeum in 1822, Hodgson *(68)* records that George Gibson's workmen were

*68* The Mithraeum re-excavated by Bosanquet in 1898. It was the first Roman building at Housesteads to be properly investigated by Hodgson in 1822. The sculptures recovered at that time are now in the Museum of Antiquities, Newcastle. *Hadrian's Wall Archive*

permitted to dig up 'any loose stones or old walls on condition that they neither used nor destroyed any that were inscribed or carved'. Many of these stones had been removed to the Gibson's house at Minstreacres, south of Hexham, by the beginning of the nineteenth century, and were to form the core of the collection of the new Society of Antiquaries of Newcastle upon Tyne, founded in 1813, the ancestor of the Museum of Antiquities in Newcastle University.[1]

The foundation of the Society of Antiquaries, despite its name, marks the close of the antiquarian age in the history of Wall studies. The emphasis now was on archaeology, the use of excavation not just to recover antiquities, but to investigate the history and structure of the buildings. The first and in many ways the greatest exponent of this method, was the Revd John Hodgson. While he lacked the resources of John Clayton, he was able to show the effectiveness of limited careful excavation on Hadrian's Wall, above all at Housesteads.

Archaeological excavation began at Housesteads in June 1822, following the discovery of the Mithraeum during draining work to the south-west of the fort. In the following month Hodgson opened the first trenches inside the fort to investigate the west side of the south gate. Results swiftly followed and were reported in the first volume of *Archaeologia Aeliana*, the journal of the Society of Antiquaries. Hodgson returned to the site in the 1830 to investigate the extent and anatomy of the fort. Several of the gates were examined as well as part of the granary and the baths at the end of building XV (see Chapter 9). The results of these enquiries formed part of Hodgson's history and description of Hadrian's Wall in his *History of Northumberland*, which was presented as a 173-page footnote appended to his account of the township of Thirlwall in the parish of Haltwhistle.

Not only was Hodgson the first to show convincingly that the Wall was built by Hadrian, but in his *History* and in the volumes of notebooks he was the first to systematically record in detail much of the structure of the forts and the Wall in the central sector.

The next major figure in the history of Housesteads in the nineteenth century was John Clayton *(colour plate 19)*. He was born in 1792 and died in 1890, effectively spanning the century. In his youth he knew John Hodgson and as an old man he was known to R.C. Bosanquet, the excavator of Housesteads in 1898. Clayton's family owned the Chesters by the north Tyne, including Chesters fort and, from an early age he developed a devotion to the Roman Wall and its antiquities. In the 1830s he began to purchase farmland along the line of Hadrian's Wall in the central sector, including Hotbank, and in 1838, in the face of local competition, he acquired Housesteads from the Gibsons.

Clayton's purchase of Housesteads Farm marks a new stage in the history of the site. His concern for the Roman monument accorded the antiquities a substantial degree of protection and few, if any, other archaeological sites in Britain can demonstrate such a continuous history of archaeological conservation. Grazing now seems to have become the predominant form of land-use although the fort remained part of a working farm with pigsties over barrack VI marked on the 1898 plan. But Clayton's aim was not simply to preserve but also to disinter and display his antiquities. In the 1830s and '40s he was a prime mover in the redevelopment of Newcastle, indeed he was the only one of the principal developers not to go bankrupt. With the fortune he acquired he was able not only to continue buying up farms with forts and lengths of Wall, but also to begin excavations within the fort. The work was carried out in the middle decades of the century and Clayton's workmen revealed the curtain walls and gates of the fort to public view. MacLaughlan's plan of the 1850s shows the outline clearly but only the granaries are visible within the interior; further excavations occurred on part of the commandant's house and possibly the outline of building XV. Unlike Clayton's excavations at Chesters, no plan of the fort was made and the full extent of his diggings at Housesteads remains unclear. Certainly Bosanquet's workmen in 1898 encountered earlier digging and he reports them as saying 'That's no dout ald Antony's been here before us'. A reference to Clayton's foreman, Anthony Place.[2]

If Clayton himself published little of the results of his excavation, from 1848 the Newcastle schoolmaster John Collingwood Bruce *(69)* came to dominate publications and publicity on Hadrian's Wall. R.C. Bosanquet recalled of the two men that, 'while Clayton dug, Bruce wrote'. Indeed much of what was uncovered was reported by 'the Great Expounder', as Bruce came to be known, in the various editions of the *Roman Wall*. In addition much was illustrated in a series of watercolours commissioned by Bruce and later used as engravings in his publications *(70)*. These are now in the Laing Art Gallery in Newcastle.

Housesteads was not simply one of the five Wall forts owned by Clayton at his death, but came to be the centre for his 'Wall estate', as he single-handedly set

*69 Left* John Collingwood Bruce photographed standing beside the winged Victory from Housesteads, *c.*1880. *Hadrian's Wall Archive*

*70 Below* An engraving of the south-west corner of the fort showing repairs, *c.*1850. The early farmhouse can be seen in the background; see *colour plate 18*. *Collingwood-Bruce 1884, 137*

about the preservation of the Roman Wall in the central sector. An account of his life recalls that:

> To talk of preserving the Wall was useless as long as well-shaped, handy-sized stones lay ready to the hand of the farmer, and the carting away of its stones went forward merrily. The great pity of it was that it was the best portions of the Wall which were removed in this fashion, for the labourers naturally preferred to take the stones that were breast high in the standing wall to stooping and lifting them up from the ground into their carts.

Clayton set about purchasing farms along the Wall as they came on the market and almost all the lengths of Wall visible within the National Trust's estate were excavated by his workmen in the second half of the nineteenth century, indeed these restored parts of the Roman Wall have come to be known as the 'Clayton Wall'. Included in this work was the investigation of three of the best-known mile-castles along the entire line: Cawfields (42) excavated in 1848, Housesteads (37) excavated in 1853, and Castle Nick (39) excavated in the following year. At all three, Clayton was concerned to display the curtain wall and the gates, just as he was doing at Housesteads fort. The internal buildings at the last two were investigated in this century although nothing is now known of the interior of milecastle 42 at Cawfields. To supervise the work on the fort and along the Wall it is reported that Clayton used to dedicate Mondays to mural studies. Shortly after 1860 the site of the farmhouse at Housesteads was moved from below the fort to its present site (*colour plate 18*). All that now remains is the well-head enclosed within a circular wall. The new farmhouse and steading were built with weatherboards and decorated stone moulding, a more tasteful design than is often encountered in hill-farms. An unusual feature was the provision of a sunny parlour projecting to the south side of the farmhouse. Most Northumberland farmhouses at this time were normally designed as straightforward stone cubes and this rather 'architectural element' can be explained as John Clayton's own study for use on his visits to the fort. Similar decorative features also appear at Shield-on-the-Wall Farm, moved by the Clayton Estate at about the same time, from the site of milecastle 41 on the line of the Roman Wall. Both works show how Clayton was not just concerned about preserving the antiquities but that he wanted to secure the landscape setting of the Wall and its forts, an issue which remains relevant today.

Housesteads, under John Clayton's care and protection, formed a part of the estate of a 'gentleman archaeologist'. In 1898 for the first time the investigations took on a more professional character when the Newcastle Society of Antiquaries instigated excavations under the direction of Bosanquet *(71)*. In many ways he spanned the two worlds, from the gentlemen to the professional, since he was a classical archaeologist by training, but from an established Northumberland family. The Society's objective was to establish the internal topography of the fort at a time when the only other nearly complete plan of a Roman fort in Britain was

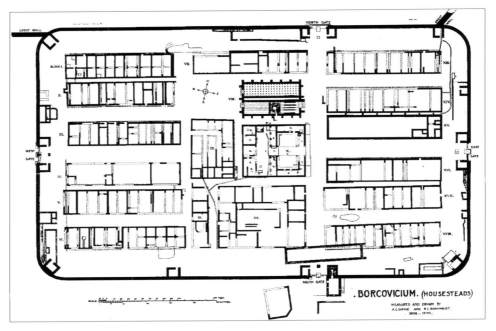

71 The first complete plan of Housesteads showing the results of Bosanquet's excavation in 1898. No attempt was made in this plan to represent the different phases of the structures.

from Birrens in Dumfriesshire. The plan of the internal buildings, on which so much of the discussion in this book is based, was established by 'tracing' the walls. That is to say the walls were located by trenches and followed. The only building fully investigated was the *principia* (termed by Bosanquet 'the *praetorium*') but he understood the limitations of his working methods and he recognised a number of different phases in the construction of the barracks. Bosanquet's report which was published six years later, remains of fundamental importance and he effectively set the agenda for all subsequent study in the twentieth century *(72)*. He was only 27 when he directed the work at Housesteads and, within a few years he became Director of the British School of Athens, where he excavated early Bronze Age sites in the Aegean. Later he was appointed as professor of Archaeology at Liverpool University but he never directly returned to Wall studies, although on his retirement he became the first secretary of the National Trust's Local Committee, before his death in 1935.[3]

The Chesters Estate, in the decades before the First World War, continued John Clayton's work of maintenance of the Roman remains at both Housesteads and along the crags, under the guidance of a young archaeologist, F.G. Simpson, an appointment referred to as 'a sort of archaeological land-agent with instructions to keep in repair the camps and so much of the wall as are on the Clayton estate'. He was to become one of the leading Wall scholars of this century and his involvement in the Estate's works ensured that for the first time there was a detailed record of the work of clearance and rebuilding of the Roman Wall on Peel Crags. As maintenance work was required at Housesteads and on milecastles 37 and 39, Simpson supervised the repairs but was also able to carry out limited, further excavations. In this way he was able to fully investigate the south-east part of the fort, including the latrines, only partly excavated in 1898 and, to examine the north-east and north-west angle towers. He was also an excellent photographer as many of the illustrations in this book show.

The beginning of the 1930s was a critical time in the history of Housesteads and the Roman Wall, not since the destruction wrought by the construction of the Newcastle to Carlisle turnpike, 'the Military Road', had the Wall faced such potential devastation. The year 1930 had opened favourably when on 3 January, *The Times* announced that Housesteads had been given by Mr J.M. Clayton to the National Trust, following the sale and dispersal of much of the Chesters Estate in the previous year[4] *(73)*. Altogether his gift comprised the fort and a length of Wall as far as milecastle 37 to the west, and to the Knag Burn Gateway to the east. The careful stewardship of the Claytons for a century, now passed to a national body. This gift did not include Housesteads Farm and, as the Trust's resources were insufficient to purchase it, Professor George Trevelyan acquired the farm with the intention that it should pass in time to the Trust. The Trevelyans of Wallington Hall in Northumberland were an old county family renowned as intellectuals and

72 Workmen from the excavations in 1898, grouped at the south gate. The young man standing behind the group in the centre is R.C. Bosanquet, then aged 27. Within a few years he was appointed Director of the British School of Athens and excavated prehistoric sites in the Aegean. Later he became professor of Archaeology at Liverpool University and, on his retirement was secretary of the Natural Trust's Committee at Housesteads.

# LOT 90

(Coloured *Yellow* on Plan No. 7).

## The Historically Important Holding

KNOWN AS

# HOUSESTEADS FARM

With substantial Farm Residence, Set of Farm Buildings and good Grazing Lands extending altogether to an Area of about

## 323a.    2r.    32p.

and including what is generally considered as

### The Most Perfect Roman Station on Hadrian's Wall

AND KNOWN AS

## BORCOVICIUM

situate on a Basaltic Precipice facing North and also including the remains of a Romano-British Town which grew up under the protection of the almost impregnable Fort.

### The Farmhouse

is stone-built and slated and contains: Entrance Hall, Sitting Room, Kitchen, Dairy and Wash-house, Two Bed Rooms. Outside Coal House.

### The Farmbuildings

consist of Piggery, Stable for 2, Three-stall Stable, Hay House, Byre for 10, Calf House for 4, Implement Shed.

Situate in No. 72 on Plan are Hay House and Byre for 12.

#### SCHEDULE.

| No. on Plan. | Description. | | Acreage. | Total Acreage. |
|---|---|---|---|---|
| | **TOWNSHIP OF THORNGRAFTON.** | | | |
| 43 | Pasture | | 22.109 | |
| 45 | Pasture | | 35.685 | |
| 47 | Pasture | | 2.536 | |
| 48 | House, Buildings, etc. | | .739 | |
| 50 | Pasture | | 113.769 | |
| 70 | Pasture | | 78.073 | |
| 71 | Pasture | | 10.403 | |
| 72 | Pasture | | 45.829 | |
| | **TOWNSHIP OF HAYDON.** | | | |
| 69 | Pasture | | 3.724 | |
| 71 | Pasture | | .583 | |
| 44 | Roman Camp | | 5.113 | |
| | Let to Mrs. H. and Mr. W. Thompson. | | | 318.623 |
| 68 | Plantation | | 1.442 | |
| 70 | Plantation | | 1.722 | |
| | **TOWNSHIP OF THORNGRAFTON.** | | | |
| 46 | | | 1.916 | |
| | In Hand. | | | 5.080 |
| | | Total Acreage ... | | 323.703 |

The Farm is let to Mrs. H. and Mr. W. Thompson with Lot 89 (Moss Kennels) on a Yearly (12th May) Tenancy at a Rental of

## £350 per annum.

The Shooting is let to Sir H. D. Blackett, Bart., at a very low Rental. Apportioned Shooting Rent £5.

The Vendor employes a caretaker for the Roman Fort with Residence in Housesteads Farm-house.

Commuted Tithe Rent Charge (Vicar of Haltwhistle), £11 6s.
(Sir H. D. Blackett, Bart.), £7 2s.

*73* Auction schedule for Housesteads farm, 1929. The Clayton estate was sold in that year and five Roman forts came under the auctioneer's hammer. The farm at Housesteads failed to achieve its reserve price and in January 1930 the fort was presented to the National Trust. In the same year the farm, including the *vicus*, was bought by Professor G.M. Trevelyan.

socialists. Not only was Professor Trevelyan a vice-chairman of the National Trust, but in the following year he became the first President of the Youth Hostels Association and a patron of their early hostel at Once Brewed. The farm at Housesteads was eventually purchased by the National Trust from his heirs in 1974.

Despite the praise in *The Times* in January about securing Housesteads for the nation, only three months later there arose one of the most serious threats ever to the Roman Wall in the central sector, which activated a remarkable display of establishment support for the archaeology of the Wall and its landscape. There had been large-scale whinstone quarries on the Whin Sill since the late nineteenth century. A section of the Wall and turret 45B were destroyed near the fort at Carvoran at the turn of the century by the workings at Walltown, and further quarrying continued until the 1920s at Cawfields, taking with it a section of Wall on the west side of the hill. The present danger arose from the acquisition of the mineral rights for much of the central sector west of Housesteads, including the farm at Hotbank, by Mr J. Wake of Darlington. His company, which for archaeologists had the sinister name 'Roman Stone Limited', planned to develop a quarry for road-building stone at Shield-on-the-Wall, close to the farmhouse John Clayton had built beside the *Vallum*. This project had the advantage of a close link with the railway line at Melkridge in the Tyne Valley. In addition, Mr Wake was sure of at least local support since Haltwhistle, the closest town, had been devastated by the closure of its coal pits and over 800 men were unemployed. A contemporary survey included it among the four most deprived towns in Britain and Mr Wake's developments promised to create 500 new jobs.

Whatever the local benefits, the national response was resounding in its opposition to the new quarry. The first news of the plan was announced in *The Times* on 11 April 1930, under the headline 'Hadrian's Wall – Quarry threat to Countryside – Strong protest by Antiquaries'. The report that followed outlined the proposed extraction of 200,000 tons of whinstone per year in the neighbourhood of Shield-on-the-Wall, Peel Crags and Housesteads. It claimed that altogether a total of a thousand million tons could be extracted over 40 years. At the least there was to be a clash of economic and historical interests. In *The Times* of the following day came a robust letter against the proposals from the Classical Association, the first of many which filled the correspondence columns of the newspaper for the next month and a half. In less than a week it was announced that Mr Lansbury, First Commissioner for the Office of Works, would visit the Wall, accompanied by the Town Clerk of Newcastle. He visited on 23 April, barely 12 days after the first report, such was the Establishment outcry. As a minister in a minority Labour government, he was met by representatives of Haltwhistle Labour Party lobbying for the 500 jobs which the scheme promised. But he was also accompanied by two of the leading Wall scholars of the period, F.G. Simpson and Parker Brewis. They left the Commissioner in little doubt of the devastation which the quarry and its plant would leave on the landscape. The Wall had been scheduled as an ancient monument for the first time the year before and Mr Wake, the developer, had accepted that it was a monument protected by government legislation. Instead he proposed to quarry beside it, leaving the Wall intact where it was visible. The Commissioner was told that 'it was the contention of the antiquaries that the Wall would be left on an unscalable knife edge, with a 400ft drop on either side'. Mr Wake was restrained for the moment, and in parliament Mr Lansbury stated that the government had 'come to the conclusion that if the quarrying could be confined to a limited area... no serious harm would be done'.

At the beginning of July many of the interested archaeologists gathered in Newcastle for the decennial Pilgrimage of the Roman Wall. There is no mention in R.G. Collingwood's *Book of the Pilgrimage* of the recent or continuing anxieties about the Wall's future. One pilgrim, Sir George Macdonald, renowned as one of the principal investigators of the Antonine Wall in Scotland, was discomfited by what he saw and composed a stirring report for *The Scotsman* on 7 July. Writing of the proposed quarrying he said: 'Unless the plague be stayed, the Pilgrims of 1940 will find that their way leads through the Valley of humiliation. It will be too late then to remember that at the end of this Valley is another, called the Valley of the Shadow of Death.' Although his words were prophetic in another sense and the next Pilgrimage could not be held until 1949, Macdonald was amongst a group of eminent men, including Rudyard Kipling and John Buchan who composed a letter to *The Times* on 29 July. They wrote that while they rejoiced 'to know that the fort at Housesteads had been handed over to the National Trust', they felt 'profound uneasiness' over the continuing intention of Roman Stone Limited to exploit the mineral rights so close to Housesteads. Their letter continued to express 'concern over disfigurement of the adjacent landscape'. This was an important step in the recognition that the archaeological remains were significant in their setting and not simply as an isolated monument, as Mr Wake had argued.

Stirred by this blast from the Establishment, Lansbury agreed to organise a conference with archaeologists and interested Members of Parliament, to help preserve the remains of the Wall and to pass legislation to strengthen the Ancient Monuments Act. This was held at Westminster on 4 November and the Amending Act was passed by Parliament on 11 June 1931, with the intention of 'preserving ancient monuments themselves, but also their surroundings'. Parliamentary legislation now secured, in the words of the Hexham poet W.W. Gibson, which were quoted at the time: 'Hadrian's Wall that strides from hill to hill, Along the wave crest of the Great Whin Sill'. But quarrying continued at Walltown and a further extension was only prevented by a government order and costly compensation in 1943. This was later reinforced by a further amendment which ensured the strict preservation of a strip of land approximately one mile wide, enclosing the Wall and the *Vallum* from Greenhead eastwards to a point to the west of Chesters, the eastern limit of the National Park today.

Another issue which then emerged in the debate for the first time was the creation of a Roman Wall National Park. National Parks came on to the government's agenda in 1929 with a paper from the Council for the Preservation of Rural England. A pamphlet proposing 'A National Park for Housesteads by Hadrian's Wall' was written by Dr Vaughan Cornish in 1931. He suggested a national park nine miles long by five broad with Housesteads as its middle point. This would comprise the sweeping Northumbrian landscape, the Roman remains and the Whin Sill, which he described as 'a geological monument which should be scheduled along with these of human history, and preserved inviolate'. Part of Cornish's enthusiasm for the Roman Wall stemmed from his thesis that it was a constituent of a trans-continental 'isothermal frontier', which had left its mark in the Great Wall of China and Hadrian's Wall. Despite these eccentricities of historical geography, the concept of a Roman Wall Park was widely accepted and formed one of the first areas presented by the National Parks Committee in 1947 as the basis of the National Parks.

There had been no archaeological work at Housesteads since before the First World War and, in the first two years following acquisition of the site the National Trust began work inside the fort and to the Wall through Housesteads Wood to the west. The clearance of the Wall was the last example of the preservation of any its length using the methods which John Clayton had first introduced. The initial project by the National Trust was the clearance of the granaries which had only been partly investigated by Bosanquet. The work was undertaken by the Durham University Excavation Committee and directed by Mr (later Professor) Eric Birley, who had become a neighbour as he had recently acquired the fort and house at Vindolanda at the Clayton sale. Little was published about this work but in the next year attention turned to the *vicus* or civil settlement outside the fort *(74)*, on land recently acquired by Professor G.M. Trevelyan. Three seasons of work produced for the first time details about the stone-built *vicus* and, in 1934 included the dramatic discovery of the 'murder house' with its skeletons buried below the floor of a living room. The excavations raised many questions about the relationship between the fort and the surrounding population, many of which remain unresolved. Another consequence of these excavations was to 'create' finds which needed housing. The old connection with the Chesters estate and its Museum was now severed and a new site museum was built by the National Trust, on land given for the purpose by Professor Trevelyan. The new museum was constructed on the same ground plan as the 'murder house', and was a very successful attempt to replicate a Roman building, even if this information is concealed from most visitors.

In addition to the excavations in the *vicus*, the National Trust also invited the Durham University Excavation Committee to investigate the interior of milecastle 37, which was fully excavated in 1933 by Peter Hunter Blair. At that time there was very close contact between the principal research body on the Wall (the Durham University Excavation Committee which comprised both Durham University and Armstrong College, Newcastle), and the management of the fort. When the Trust took over Housesteads, the management was the responsibility of a local committee of prominent figures, with Professor R.C. Bosanquet as its

*74* Outlet for the latrine sewer at the south-east angle of the fort, from the excavations by Professor Eric Birley in 1931. *Hadrian's Wall Archive*

secretary. On his death in 1935 he was succeeded by Eric Birley of Durham University, who remained secretary until the site was transferred to the guardianship of the Ministry of Works in 1951. Other changes during this period were the removal of a perimeter wall around the headquarters at the time of Queen Mary's visit in 1935 and, the demolition of the central part of the late medieval long house inside the south gate, on the mistaken belief that it was a nineteenth-century building. By 1935 the numbers of visitors had risen to 15,000 per year so it is not surprising there was provision of earth closets in the farm buildings.

Any attempt to continue the momentum of research in the 1930s was prevented by the outbreak of war in 1939 and the only research was the location of turret 36B in 1945 by F.G. Simpson, thus establishing that the building of some of the turrets and milecastles preceded the construction of the fort itself. The war brought about wider social and economic changes throughout the nation which were reflected even at Housesteads. Until the outbreak of war the National Trust for Places of Historic Interest or Natural Beauty was primarily seen as an organisation concerned with open space properties such as the fells of the Lake District, but the decline in the fortunes of many of the owners of historic houses, especially during the war years, brought about the introduction of the 'Country House Scheme' which was to radically alter the Trust's priorities and consequently the way it was perceived by the nation. Its primary post-war role was to become the guardian of the English country house. In accordance with this, many of its major archaeological properties were given into the care and guardianship of the Ministry of Public Buildings and Works which was deemed to be a body with greater expertise in the management of archaeological sites. On Hadrian's Wall this move was welcomed by the leading Wall scholars, including Professors Ian Richmond and Eric Birley. Among the other monuments that changed management at this time were Castlerigg Stone Circle and Avebury, both of which were returned to the Trust's control in 1994.

## NEW WALLS FOR OLD: A CONFLICT OF CONSERVATION METHODOLOGIES

The change in management at Housesteads occurred in 1951 and for nearly a decade the Ministry were principally concerned with the consolidation of the Roman masonry exposed and restored by Clayton and his successors. For over a century the Chesters Estate and their successors, the National Trust, had established clear methods for the conservation of what has come to be known as the Clayton Wall. The Roman Wall was excavated of its accumulated tumble and the fallen facing stones were set aside. These were re-laid dry in level courses on the surviving wall and core, without the use of mortar or cement. New core was built up using some of the small rubble left from the clearance. The new facing was laid level on both sides and the top was then capped with turf, taken from the adjacent grassland. This method only used materials available on site and was therefore inexpensive and could be carried out by estate workmen skilled in the building of dry-stone walls. When the work was carried out carefully, as on Peel Crags under the supervision of F.G. Simpson in 1910, it survives remarkably well and the untouched original Roman core and facing are largely unaffected and can be readily seen with scarcely any modern intrusion. Other lengths of Clayton Wall, in particular parts of Hotbank Crags, present a less impressive monument, with irregular facing and an unstable core, since the method is most successful on relatively level ground such as the tops of the crags.

In the 1950s the immediate problem confronting the Ministry of Works was how to conserve the walls of Housesteads restored by the Clayton method and, to ensure the maintenance of what was already a popular tourist site. Since the turn of the century the Ministry, and their predecessors the Office of Works, had adopted a different approach for the preservation of ancient monuments. Founded on the tenets of the Arts and Crafts Movement, the underlying philosophy was to consolidate walls and ruins as found. No new stonework was to be added and any restoration should be kept to an absolute minimum, and should be easily recognisable for what it was. It should be possible to 'read' a monument and easily distinguish original work from recent interventions. This method is normally called consolidation and had been used by Ministry's works staff on lengths of Hadrian's Wall since the 1930s.

By the 1950s the National Trust and the Ministry of Works were responsible for various stretches of Wall of about equal length, 3½ miles each, and there was a major programme of consolidation by the Ministry on Walltown Crags. With the support of the leading Wall archaeologists, the Ministry's Inspectorate of

Ancient Monuments felt that it should gradually assume guardianship over the whole 80 miles and preserve it in a uniform manner as 'the importance of the great monument warrants'. Such a view was not, however, accepted by the Trust and a dispute arose in 1957 concerning the methods of the preservation and presentation of the Wall, a debate still relevant today when the future of the Wall is bound up in World Heritage Sites and National Trails.

The dispute between the Trust and the Ministry was resolved in 1957, but in the following year a newspaper article revived the issues and opened a public debate which was not quietened until there had been a debate in Parliament. The instigator was Jacquetta Hawkes *(75)*, an archaeologist, journalist and wife of the novelist J.B. Priestly, who visited the Wall in February and wrote in *The Observer* article under the provocative title of the 'Battle of Hadrian's Wall', unofficially championing the Trust's methods of preservation. Alone among the archaeologists of her time, Hawkes challenged the methods used by the Ministry. She wrote of the recent dispute between the Trust and the Ministry:

> If the clash were simply between a romantic policy of laissez faire and a realistic acceptance of the drastic measures to preserve the Wall for posterity, then judgement would have to given in favour of restoration, even though it meant some loss of beauty and atmosphere.

What had vexed the local agent of the Trust the previous year and what Mrs Hawkes now took up, concerned not just the presentation of the Wall, but the methods used to consolidate it. The opponents of the Ministry felt that in the process of preservation, which was carried out without archaeological supervision, the detailed evidence of 'repairs and alterations were destroyed without record'. Furthermore the wall that emerged from the consolidation was 'not Hadrian's Wall at all. It is a copy – and one that has lost all the gifts of time.'[5]

The archaeological establishment in the northern universities supported the Ministry to a man in rejecting these criticisms and these real issues of the conservation and preservation of the Wall were not properly addressed until the 1980s when the importance of preserving the Roman mortars was appreciated. It was to be nearly another 25 years before archaeologists were employed to observe and record the Roman Wall during consolidation; a welcome return to the professional standards set by the Chesters Estate and their archaeological land-agent, F.G. Simpson in the years before the First World War.

Archaeological research inside the fort in the 1950s and '60s set about the investigation of the development of the barracks only hinted at by Bosanquet. Barracks XIV and building XV were examined and displayed. Later attention turned to the display of the central range buildings, including the commandant's house and the hospital. By the early 1970s, Housesteads was the only fort on Hadrian's Wall where it was possible to see excavated examples of all the different types of internal buildings.

75 Jaquetta Hawkes and 'Cubby'
Ackland (the National Trust land
agent) on the Wall west of
Housesteads, 1957. *The National Trust*

From 1974-81, excavations continued in the north-east corner including
barrack XIII as well as the ramparts and roads in the segment between the north
and east gates. The north-east corner of the fort is now laid out to display the
fourth century appearance of the interior. The most recent excavation took place
in 1984 on part of the north curtain wall and, this revealed a complex sequence
of structural phases against the north curtain and the remains of an early road
leading out of the north gate.

Housesteads today remains the most popular site on Hadrian's Wall, managed
by English Heritage and owned by the National Trust. After over 50 years of co-
habitation between the two organisations there are now proposals for joint
management of the archaeological site in its landscape, which is a worthy
ambition. It is only to be hoped that these and other national and local bodies can
live up to the expectations expressed by William Stuckeley at the end of his tour
of Roman antiquities in the north:

> The amazing scene of Roman grandeur in Britain which I beheld this journey,....
> the more I despaired of conveying it to the reader.... Yet I hold myself obliged to
> preserve as well as I can, the memory of such things as I saw; which, added to what
> future times will discover, will revive the Roman glory among us.... The tribute at
> least we owe them, and they deserve it at our hands, to preserve their remains.

# VISITING HOUSESTEADS

## HOUSESTEADS FORT AND MUSEUM

The fort, *vicus* and museum are in the care of English Heritage and can be visited throughout the year. The fields around the fort are owned and managed by the National Trust and there is public access to the two fields between the car park and Hadrian's Wall. It is important to remember that these fields are grazed throughout the year, so dogs should always be kept on a lead, especially at lambing in April.

Sites to visit in the immediate vicinity of the fort include the Knag Burn Gate, the baths in the valley of the Knag Burn, Chapel Hill and the Roman Wall to the north of it *(66)*.

By the car park is a visitor centre run by the National Trust and Northumberland National Park, with a display about the archaeology of the National Trust's Hadrian's Wall estate.

## WEST OF HOUSESTEADS

The major sites to be seen between Housesteads and Steel Rigg, from east to west, are as follows:

Housesteads milecastle (37), Hadrian's Wall on Housesteads and Cuddy's Crags, the site of milecastle 38 at Hotbank, the Romano-British native settlement at Milking Gap, Hadrian's Wall from Highshield Crags to Castle Nick, Castle Nick milecastle (39) and the sheilings to the east of Castle Nick. Another native settlement between the Wall and Bradley farm is difficult to locate.

Throughout this length the Military Way is very well preserved, especially to the south of Cuddy's Crags and Highshield Crags. Traces of a Bronze Age field boundary are visible to the south of Sycamore Gap, at one point cut by the Military Way.

West of Cat Stairs the Wall is exceptionally well preserved on Peel Crags before the steep descent into Peel Gap and the site of Peel Gap tower. The position of the turret on Peel Crags (39a) is clearly marked by large blocks in the face of Hadrian's Wall.

South of the Military Way, the medieval settlement at Bradley Green can be seen from a public footpath running south towards Grandey's Knowe.

An additional and rewarding walk follows one of the footpaths north of the Wall to view Housesteads from the north.

EAST OF HOUSESTEADS

The Wall itself is not visible beyond the valley of the Knag Burn, but the site of milecastle 36 can be seen on the isolated King's Hill. Further along, the line of the Wall falls into a wide gap known as Busy Gap, with a narrow gate called the King's Wicket. On the north side is a medieval earthwork. From here the Wall climbs up to Sewingshields Crag and the visible remains of turret 35a and the Sewingshields milecastle (35). For the walker, the new Hadrian's Wall Trail continues east towards Carrawburgh Fort, past the well preserved turrets, 34a and 33b.

Housesteads Museum contains only a small collection of objects found in recent excavations on the fort and *vicus*. The main collection of sculptures, inscriptions and artefacts from the site are in the Chesters Museum (John Clayton's collection) and in the Museum of Antiquities, University of Newcastle upon Tyne.

# GLOSSARY

*ala* A wing of cavalry in the Roman army – normally of a size around 500 strong, to occupy a normal auxiliary fort (e.g., Chesters)

**architrave** Formalised lintel in stone or timber carried from the top of one column or pier to another

**ashlar** Masonry of large blocks dressed to even faces and square edges

**auxiliary** A Roman soldier in a unit other than a legion

**Broad Wall** The module or gauge of Hadrian's Wall as first built, around 10ft (2.8m) thick

**century/***centuria* A century of infantry soldiers, normally with a paper strength of between 80-100 men, and commanded by a centurion. A century is the size of unit to be accommodated in a single infantry barrack block

**chamfer** Surface formed by cutting off a square edge, usually at an angle of 45 degrees

**clerestory** Upper storey of walls pierced by windows, often applied to the nave walls of a church

**cohort/***cohors* A unit of infantry – though there were also mixed cohorts – either of single strength (around 500) or double strength (around 1,000 men strong)

**contubernium** *(-a plural)* Single compartments within barrack blocks, suitable for the accommodation of 8-10 men and their equipment

**crenellation** Battlements along the top of a defensive wall to provide protection for men posted on its top

*cuneus* Literally a wedge, used as the name for a unit of German irregular troops. It could be derived from the German practice of fighting in wedge-shaped formations

*forum* The centre of a Roman town, incorporating public spaces and market area, normally a large, rectangular open space

**headers and stretchers** Stone blocks laid alternately at right angles and along the line of a wall

**impost blocks** A block placed between the capital of a column or pier and the arch or vault it supports

**intervallum street** Road running parallel with the fort between the barracks and the rampart bank

**jamb** Side post of a door or window

**legion/***legio* The elite troops of the Roman army. Legions were some 6,000 strong and normally not posted to ordinary 'frontier' duties. They contained specialist units of builders

**loop** Narrow vertical opening in a wall to admit light or air

**merlons** Upward projections between the openings or embrasures of the parapet

**milecastle** A small walled fortlet incorporating gateways to the north and south linked by a central roadway, provided at approximate intervals of one Roman mile for the whole length of Hadrian's Wall. Modern convention numbers these from 0 (at Wallsend) to 80 (at Bowness, Cumbria)

**mullion** Vertical member in a window opening

**Narrow Wall** Hadrian's Wall as completed and as in parts rebuilt was not finished to the original Broad Wall specification. Narrow Wall signifies those portions finished to a narrower gauge

**portico** A porch, open on one side with a row of columns supporting the roof

**principia** The headquarters building within a Roman fort. Set at its centre, this consisted of a courtyard, a lofty hall set across the width of the building, and a series of offices opening off it

**quoins** Dressed stone at the angles of a building

**reiver** A sixteenth-century rustler and robber in the Anglo-Scottish borderland

**respond** Half-pier bonded with a wall and carrying one end of an arch or lintel

**return** The side or part which falls away at right angles from the front or direct line of a structure

**springer** The large stones at the top of a gate-jamb from which the gate arch begins

**string course** Intermediate stone course or moulding projecting from the surface of a wall

**tail-bedded** The term describes facing stones, their external face left relatively free of mortar, but their inner portions (or 'tails') set in the core of a wall for stability

*tribunal* A platform within the hall of a headquarters building in a Roman fort

**tufa** Soft porous stone often used in the vaulted roofs of Roman baths, either calcareous or volcanic in origin

**turf wall** The portions of Hadrian's Wall west of the River Irthing at Willowford which were originally built in turf rather than stone

**turret** A small rectangular tower, spaced between milecastles at intervals of a third of a Roman mile. Modern convention numbers these in sequence from the east end of the Wall – 0A, 0B, 1A, 1B and so on, taking their number from the milecastle to their east

*vallum* A flat-bottomed ditch flanked by mounds running to the south of Hadrian's Wall for much of its length. Sometimes nearby, and sometimes as much as half a mile away, it appears to delimit a military zone

**vexillation** A special task-force of Roman troops gathered from several units, or subdivided from a unit; normally a portion of a legion

*vicani* Collective term for the civilians living in the *vicus* next to a Roman fort

*vicus* The settlement, normally of civilians, clustered round many Roman forts

**voussoir** A wedge-shaped stone forming part of an arch

**wall-walk** A footpath or platform provided along the top of a defensive wall, especially the curtain wall

**windowhead** Single stone lintel, often arched in form

**wing** see *ala*

# NOTES

ACKNOWLEDGEMENTS

1    Rushworth, A. (ed.) (forthcoming) *The Grandest Station: Excavation and Survey at Housesteads Roman Fort by C.M. Daniels, J.P. Gillam, J.G. Crow, D. J. Smith and the RCHME 1954-88*. English Heritage Archaeological Report, London.

CHAPTER 1

1    For references to early antiquaries see Bosanquet 1904, 193-99; Birley 1961.
2    For the background to the building of the Wall see Breeze and Dobson 2002; Crow 2004; and Breeze forthcoming.
3    The building of the Wall, see note 2 above and especially Breeze (forthcoming).

CHAPTER 2

1    Breeze and Hill 2001, but see the comments in Bidwell 2003 reasserting the traditional view of a Tyneside origin for the construction of the Wall.
2    See Daniels 1978, 140 for a plan showing the location of the turret and the line of the Broad foundation.
3    For example Jones and Wooliscroft 2001, 79; see the comments in Crow 2004, 121–30
4    Jones and Wooliscroft 2001, plate 24; Blair 1934.
5    However, see Breeze 2003 who reviews the evidence for warfare in Britain under Hadrian and the implications for the building history of the Wall.

6    For the evidence of farming and settlement underlying Roman forts and the Wall, see most recently Hodgson *et al.* 2001.
7    For quarries in the central sector see Crow 1991; the kiln at Housesteads is published in Simpson 1976.
8    Bruce 1884, 127.

CHAPTER 3

1    For Hadrian's frontier policy see Birley T. 1997; and Whittaker 2000.
2    For Roman forts see Breeze 1983 and Bidwell 1997.
3    Bidwell 1997, plate 5.
4    See the detailed discussion of the gates and other stone buildings at Housesteads in Taylor 2000; the stonework is discussed in detail in Hill forthcoming.

CHAPTER 4

1    Bosanqet 1904; Wilkes 1960,1961, Barrack XIV and building XV; Charlesworth 1975, 1976, *Praetorium* and Hospital; Smith *Principia*, Daniels and Gillam *Barrack XIII in Rushworth* forthcoming.
2    Bowman 1998.
3    Charlesworth 1971B.

CHAPTER 5

1    For a discussion of the Roman name of Housesteads see Rivet and Smith 1979.
2    Bowman 1998.
3    Breeze 2003; Birley 1998

4 A recent study of Housesteads Ware and its Frisian origins questions this identification with Twente and observes that the known distribution of 'Frisian' pottery is not found in this area of Holland

CHAPTER 6

1 The standard discussion of Housesteads ware remains Jobey 1979. I am grateful to Jose Peters for access to her unpublished study which includes thin section analysis of selected sherds. The evidence from Birdoswald is summarised in Wilmott 2001, 109.
2 Salway 1967, 207-60.
3 The geophysical survey at Halton Chesters indicates clearly the line of the *Vallum* below the *vicus* buildings, Taylor *et al.* 2000; The dating evidence from Birdoswald is discussed by Wilmott 2001, 82-83 and the filling of the *Vallum* can be dated after the 150s.
4 See the recent discussion in Hanson 2004 and Hingley 2004.

CHAPTER 7

1 More detailed discussion of building XV and the other late Roman buildings at Housesteads can be found in Rushworth forthcoming.

CHAPTER 8

For a recent discussion of the late Roman army in Britain see Southern 2004.
1 See the detailed discussion of the barracks XIII and XIV and the north-east rampart in Rushworth forthcoming.
2 See Bidwell 1997, 62-67; although similarities of plan can be seen, there are significant variations in size between many of the barracks discussed.
3 Crow 1988.

4 For a recent discussion of the Roman army in Britain see Southern 2004.
5 See Rushworth forthcoming.

CHAPTER 9

1 See Birley 2003 for a summary of the evidence for Christianity at Vindolanda.
2 See Smith 1996 for possible churches in northern Britain; the evidence for most of these is less convincing than the two examples from Housesteads and Vindolanda discussed here.
3 The evidence for medieval settlement and land use is discussed in Woodside and Crow 1999.
4 See the map of medieval settlement and boundaries in Woodside and Crow 1999, fig. 29.
5 See Welfare in Rushworth forthcoming for a detailed discussion of the medieval and early modern field systems and landholdings at Housesteads.
6 Housesteads in the seventeenth century is discussed in greater detail in Woodside and Crow 1999, 71.

CHAPTER 10

1 The fullest history of the antiquarian visits and early excavations can be found in the introduction to R.C. Bosanquet's report (1904), see also Birley 1961, 178-84 and Woodside and Crow 1999, 96ff.
2 For Clayton Hadrian's Wall Estate see Woodside and Crow 1999, 84ff; 102-04.
3 Bosanquet 1904.
4 See also the *Illustrated London News* for a double-page illustrated spread celebrating the Trust's acquisition of the fort.
5 I am grateful to colleagues in English Heritage and the National Trust for access to files concerning the issues about consolidation in the 1950s.

# BIBLIOGRAPHY

ABBREVIATIONS

*AA Archaeologia Aeliana.*

*CSIR* J.C. Coulston and E.J. Phillips (1988) *Corpus Signorum Imperii Romani.* Vol. 1, fasc. 6, Oxford

*CW* Transactions of the Cumberland and Westmorland Antiquarian and Archaeological Society

*PSAN* Proceedings of the Society of Antiquaries of Newcastle upon Tyne

*RIB* R.G. Collingwood and R.P. Wright (1965) *The Roman Inscriptions of Britain.* Vol. 1, Oxford


GENERAL BIBLIOGRAPHY

Bidwell, P. 1997 *Roman forts in Britain* (London)

Birley, A.R. 1997 *Hadrian, the Restless Emperor* (London)

Birley, A.R. 2002 *Garrison life at Vindolanda, a Band of Brothers* (Stroud)

Bowman, A.K. 1998 *Life and Letters on Hadrian's Wall* (London)

Breeze, D.J. and Dobson, B. 2000 *Hadrian's Wall* (4th ed. London)

Breeze, D.J. and Hill, P.R. 2002 'Hadrian's Wall began here', *Archaeologia Aeliana* 5, 29, 1-2.

Crow, J.G. 1986 'The function of Hadrian's Wall and the comparative evidence of Late Roman Long Walls', in: *Studien zur Militärgrenzen Roms III (13 Internationaler Limes Kongress Aalen 1983)* (Stuttgart) 724-9.

Crow, J.G. 1991 'A review of current research on the turrets and curtain of Hadrian's Wall', *Britannia* 22, 51-63.

Crow J. 2004 The Northern Frontier of Britain from Trajan to Antoninus Pius; Roman Builders and Native Britains in Todd (2004), p.144-145

Daniels, C.M. 1978 *Handbook to the Roman Wall* (13th ed. Newcastle upon Tyne)

Henig M. (1984) *Religion in Roman Britain* (London)

Hodgson, N. Stobbs G.C. and van der Veen M. 2001 'An Iron-Age Settlement and Remains of Earlier Prehistoric Date beneath South Shields Roman Fort, Tyne and Wear' *Archaeological Journal* 158, 62-100

Jones, G B.D. and Wooliscroft, D. 2001 *Hadrian's Wall from the Air* (Stroud)

Maxwell, G.S., 1998 *A Gathering of the Eagles, Scenes from Roman Scotland* (Edinburgh)

Southern, P. (2004) 'The Army in late Roman Britain' in Todd (2004), 393-408

Taylor, D.J.A., Robinson, J., Biggins, J.A. 2000 'A report on a geophysical survey of the Roman fort and *vicus* at Halton Chesters', *Archaeologia Aeliana* 5, 28, 37-46

Todd, M. (ed.) (2004) *A companion to Roman Britain* (Oxford)

Welfare, H. and Swan, V. 1995 *Roman Camps in England, the Field Archaeology,* (RCHME, London)

Wilmott, Tony 2001, *Birdoswald Roman Fort, 1800 years on Hadrian's Wall* (Stroud)

Whittaker, C.R. 2000 'Frontiers', in A.K. Bowman, P. Garnsey and D. Rathbone, (edd.) *The High Empire, A.D. 70-192, The Cambridge Ancient History* XI ( 2nd ed. Cambridge).

## HOUSESTEADS BIBLIOGRAPHY

*A full bibliography of Housesteads is identical to a general bibliography of Hadrian's Wall, since the site is never ignored. The following is a list of those works which contain original information specific to Housesteads used in the preparation of this book.*

Abbatt, R. (1849) *A History of the Picts' or Romano-British Wall, and of the Roman Stations and Vallum.* (27ff) London

*AA,* 6 (1865) 200 ('Roman coins found at Borcovicus'); 225 ('Fibulae from Borcovicus')

Barrow, G. (1989) 'Settlement on the Anglo-Scottish Borders', in, R. Bartlett and A. MacKay, *Medieval Frontier Societies* (Oxford) 3-21.

Bidwell, P.T. (ed.) (1999) *Hadrian's Wall 1989-1999:A Summary of Recent Excavations and Research prepared for the Twelfth Pilgrimage of Hadrian's Wall, 14-21 August 1999.* Cumberland and Westmorland Antiquarian and Archaeological Society and the Society of Antiquaries of Newcastle upon Tyne, Carlisle.

Birley, E., Charlton, J. and Hedley W. P. (1932) 'Excavations at Housesteads in 1931', *AA,* 9, 222-237

Birley, E., Charlton J. and Hedley, W. P. (1933) 'Excavations at Housesteads in 1932', *AA,* 10, 82-96

Birley, E. and Charlton, J. (1934) 'Third Report on Excavations at Housesteads', *AA,* 11, 185-205

Birley, E. and Keeney, G.S. (1935) 'Fourth Report on Excavations at Housesteads', *AA,* 12, 204-258

Birley, E. (1936) *Housesteads, Northumberland: Fort Milecastle and Settlement.* Housesteads Management Committee, the National Trust

Birley, E. (1937) 'Fifth Report on Excavations at Housesteads', *AA,* 14, 172-184

Birley, E. (1937-1938) 'A modern building at Housesteads', *PSAN,* 8, 191-193

Birley, E. (1952) *Housesteads Roman Fort, Northumberland.* HMSO, Ministry of Works Official Guidebook

Birley, E. (1961) *Research on Hadrian's Wall.* Kendal

Birley, E. (1962) 'Sir John Clerk's visit to the North of England in 1724', *Transactions of the Architectural and Archaeological Society of Durham and Northumberland,* 11, pts 3-4, 221-246

Birley, E. (1974) 'Cohors I Tungrorum and the oracle of Clarian Apollo', *Chiron,* 4, 511-513

Birley, R.E. (1961) 'Housesteads civil settlement, 1960', *AA,* 39, 301-319

Birley, R.E. (1962) 'Housesteads *vicus,* 1961', *AA,* 40, 117-133

Blagg, T.F.C. (1985) 'A relief carving of two female figures from Housesteads', *AA,* 13, 1-5

Blair, Hunter F. (1934) 'Housesteads Milecastle', *AA*, 11, 103-120

Bosanquet, R.C. (1898) 'Excavations at Housesteads', *PSAN*, 8, 247-254

Bosanquet, R.C. (1904) Excavations on the line of the Roman Wall in Northumberland: 1. The Roman Camp at Housesteads', *AA*, 25, 193ff

Bosanquet, R.C. (1922A) 'On an altar dedicated to the Alaisiagae', *AA*, 19, 185-196

Bosanquet, R.C. (1922B) 'A newly discovered centurial stone at Housesteads', *AA*, 19, 198-9

Bosanquet, R.C. (1925) 'Annual meeting 1925, Newcastle upon Tyne 21-29 July', *Archaeological Journal*, 82, 222-223

Bosanquet, R.C. (1929) 'Dr John Lingard's notes on the Roman Wall', *AA*, 6, 130-162

Bosanquet, R.C. and Birley, E. (ed.) (1955) 'Robert Smith and the "Observations upon the Picts Wall" (1708-9)', *CW*, 55, 154-171

Brand, J. (1789) *The History and Antiquities of the Town and County of the Town of Newcastle upon Tyne*. London

Breeze, D. (1983) *Roman Forts in Britain*. London

Bruce, J.C. (1851A) *The Roman Wall*. 1st edition; London & Newcastle upon Tyne

Bruce, J.C. (1851B) *Views on the Line of the Roman Wall in the North of England*. Newcastle upon Tyne.

Bruce, J.C. (1853) *The Roman Wall*. 2nd edition; London & Newcastle upon Tyne

Bruce, J.C. (1857) 'Visit to Cilurnum, Borcovicus etc.', *PSAN*, 1, nr. 27, 234-235

Bruce, J.C. (1863) *The Wallet Book of the Roman Wall*. London & Newcastle upon Tyne

Bruce, J.C. (1867) *The Roman Wall*, 3rd edition; London & Newcastle upon Tyne

Bruce, J.C. (1875) *Lapidarium Septentrionale, or a Description of the Monuments of Roman Rule in the North of England*. London & Newcastle upon Tyne

Bruce, J.C. (1884) *The Handbook to the Roman Wall*. 2nd edition; London & Newcastle upon Tyne

Bruce, J.C. (1885) *The Handbook to the Roman Wall*. 3rd edition; London & Newcastle upon Tyne

Budge, E.A.W. (1902) *The Roman Antiquities in the Museum at Chesters*. London

Burn, A.R. (1969) *The Romans in Britain. An Anthology of Inscriptions*. 2nd edition; Oxford

Camden, W. (1722) *Britannia* (ed. E. Gibson). London

Charlesworth, D. (1969) 'A gold signet ring from Housesteads'. *AA*, 47, 39-42

Charlesworth, D. (1971A) 'Housesteads west ditch and its relationship to Hadrian's Wall'. *AA*, 49, 95-99

Charlesworth, D. (1971B) 'A group of vessels from the commandant's house, Housesteads'. *Journal of Glass Studies*, 13, 34-37

Charlesworth, D. (1975) 'The Commandant's house, Housesteads'. *AA*, 3, 17-42

Charlesworth, D. (1976) 'The hospital, Housesteads'. *AA*, 4, 17-30

Clayton, J. (1855-1857) *PSAN*, 1, 3-5 (altar found in fort); 51-53 (Knag Burn Gate located); 186-188 (Knag Burn gate excavation)

Clayton, J., Watkin, W.T., Hubner, E. and Stephens, G. (1885) 'On the discovery of Roman inscribed altars etc., at Housesteads, November 1883'. *AA*, 10, 148-150, 169-171

Collingwood, R.G. (1930) *The Book of the Pilgrimage of Hadrian's Wall, July 1st to 4th 1930*. (33-36, fig. 6) Newcastle upon Tyne

Cornish, V. (1931) *A National Park for Housesteads by Hadrian's Wall in Northumberland*. London

Countryside Commission (1992) *The Hadrian's Wall Path proposed National Trail: Formal Consultation*. Cheltenham

Crow, J.G. (1988) 'An excavation of the north curtain wall at Housesteads', *AA*, 16, 61-124

Crow, J.G. (1989) *Housesteads Roman Fort*. English Heritage Guidebook, London

Crow, J.G. (1991) 'Construction and reconstruction in the Central Sector of Hadrian's Wall', in V.A. Maxfield & M.J. Dobson (eds.) *Roman Frontier Studies 1989*, 44-47, Exeter

Crow, J.G. (1995) *Housesteads*. English Heritage/Batsford, London

Crow, J.G. (forthcoming) 'Excavation around the fort', in A. Rushworth (ed.) *The Grandest Station: Excavation and Survey at Housesteads Roman Fort by C.M. Daniels, J.P. Gillam, J.G. Crow, D. J. Smith and the RCHME 1954-88*. English Heritage Archaeological Report, London

Crow, J.G. and Rushworth, A. (1994) *Housesteads Roman Fort and its Environs: Survey and Analysis of the Archaeological Deposits*. (Unpub. assessment report for English Heritage Historic Properties North)

Curteis, M.E. (1988) *The Coinage of Housesteads: A Numismatic Study of the Economy and Chronology of a fort on Hadrian's Wall*, unpub MA thesis, Durham University

*CW*, 15 (1899) 335-338 (Description of 1898 Society excursion to 'Borcovicus' – tour of Bosanquet's excavations)

Daniels, C.M. (1962) 'Mithras Saecularis, the Housesteads mithraeum and a fragment from Carrawburgh', *AA* 40 105-133

Daniels, C.M. (ed.) (1978) *Handbook to the Roman Wall*. 13th edition; Newcastle upon Tyne

Daniels, C. M. (1980) 'Excavation at Wallsend and the fourth-century barracks on Hadrian's Wall', in W. S. Hanson and L.J. Keppie, *Roman Frontier Studies 1979*, BAR Int Series 71(i), Oxford: 173-193

Daniels, C.M. (ed.) (1989) *The Eleventh Pilgrimage of Hadrian's Wall*. (55-59) Newcastle upon Tyne

Dornier, A. 1968 'Knag Burn, Housesteads, Northumberland', *Archaeological Newsbulletin for Northumberland, Cumberland and Westmorland*, 1 (Jan. 1968), 2-4

Dornier, A. 1969 'Knag Burn, Housesteads, Northumberland', *Archaeological Newsbulletin for Northumberland, Cumberland and Westmorland*, 4 (Jan. 1969), 5

Eden, W.A. (1937) 'The Housesteads Terraces', *Liverpool Annals of Archaeology*, 24, 156-164

Edwards, D.A. and Green, C.J.S. (1977) 'The Saxon Shore fort and settlement at Brancaster, Norfolk', in D.E. Johnston (ed.) *The Saxon Shore*. CBA Research Report 18, London: 21-29

Frere, S.S. (ed.), (1988) (Note on excavation on the terraces – J.G. Crow) 'Roman Britain in 1987: I. Sites explored', *Britannia*, 19, 434

Frere, S.S. (ed.), (1989) (Note on excavation at Knag Burn gate – J. G. Crow) in 'Roman Britain in 1988: I. Sites explored', *Britannia*, 20, 273

Frere, S.S. and St. Joseph, J.K. (1983) *Roman Britain from the air*. Cambridge

*Gentleman's Magazine* (1834) 1, p.316 (Note on Hodgson's 'elaborate report' of his excavations at Housesteads to Newcastle Society of Antiquaries)

Goodburn, R. (ed.), (1976) (Note on intervention on Knag Burn curtain – I. W. Stuart) in 'Roman Britain in 1975: I. Sites explored', *Britannia*, 7, 309

Goodburn, R. (ed.), (1978) 'Roman Britain in 1977: I. Sites explored', *Britannia* 9, 420-421

Gordon, A. (1726) *Itinerarium Septentrionale*. London

Hassall, M.W.C. and Tomlin, R.S.O. (1987) (Note on COH I TV inscription in S granary) in 'Roman Britain in 1986: II. Inscriptions', *Britannia*, 18, 369

Harrison, D. (1956) *Along Hadrian's Wall*. London

Haverfield, F.J. (1911) 'Cotton Iulius F. VI. Notes on Reginald Bainbrigg of Appelby, on William Camden and on some Roman inscriptions', *CW*, 11, 343-378

Hedley, W. P. (1931) 'Ancient cultivations at Housesteads', *Antiquity*, 5, 351-354.

Hill, P.R.(forthcoming) 'The Gateways: Technical survey of the masonry', in A. Rushworth (ed.) *The Grandest Station: Excavation and Survey at Housesteads Roman Fort by C.M. Daniels, J.P. Gillam, J.G. Crow, D.J. Smith and the RCHME 1954-88.* English Heritage Archaeological Report, London

Hodgson, J. (n.d., post 1810) *A Topographical and Historical Description of the County of Northumberland.* (in *'The Beauties of England and Wales'* series)

Hodgson, J. (1822) 'Observations on the Roman Station of Housesteads'. *AA*, 1, 263-320

Hodgson, J. (1828) *History of Northumberland*, part 3, vol. II. Newcastle upon Tyne

Hodgson, J. (1840) *History of Northumberland*, part 2, vol. III. Newcastle upon Tyne.

Horsley, J. (1732) *Britannia Romana.* London

Hunter, C. (1702) (Letter in*) Philosophical Transactions of the Royal Society*, 23, no.278, p.1131.

Hutton, W. (1802) *The History of the Roman Wall, which crosses the Island of Britain, from the German Ocean to the Irish Sea. Describing its ancient State and its Appearance in the year 1801.* London

*Illustrated London News* (18-1-1930) 'Crown of our chief Roman monument given to the nation', 84-85

*Illustrated London News* (26-4-1930) 'Hadrian's Wall and quarrying: in the threatened area', 735; 'Where Quarrying menaces our chief Roman monument' (Reconstruction of Housesteads fort), 736-737

James, S.T. (1984) 'Britain and the Late Roman Army', in T.F.C. Blagg and A.C. King (eds.) *Military and Civilian in Roman Britain.* BAR Int Ser 136, Oxford: 161-186

James, S.T. (2001) 'Soldiers and Civilians: identity and interaction in Roman Britain', in S.T. James and M.J. Millett (eds.) *Britons and Romans: advancing an archaeological agenda.* CBA Research Report 125, London: 77-89

Jobey, I. (1979) 'Housesteads Ware – A Frisian tradition on Hadrian's Wall', *AA*, 7, 127-143

Lawson, W. (1966) 'The origin of the Military Road from Newcastle to Carlisle', *AA*, 44, 185-207

Lawson, W. (1973) 'The construction of the Military Road in Northumberland 1751-1757', *AA*, 1, 177-193

Leach, J., and Wilkes, J.J. (1962) 'Excavations in the Roman fort at Housesteads, 1961', *AA*, 40, 83-96

McGowan, P. Crow. J. and Rushworth A. (2002) *Housesteads Roman Fort Conservation Plan* English Heritage/National Trust, 2 vols

MacLauchlan, H. (1857) *The Roman Wall and Illustrations of the principal Vestiges of Roman Occupation in the North of England.* London

MacLauchlan, H. (1858) *Memoir written during a Survey of the Roman Wall, through the Counties of Northumberland and Cumberland in the Years 1852-1854.* London

Mann, J.C. (1989) 'The Housesteads latrine', *AA*, 17, 1-4

National Trust (1994) *The National Trust Hadrian's Wall Estate Management Plan*

Ordnance Survey (1972) *Map of Hadrian's Wall.* Southampton

Ornsby, G. (ed.) (1878) *Selections from the Household Books of Lord William Howard of Naworth Castle.* Surtees Society, 68

Pevsner, N. (ed. J. Grundy, G. McCombie, P.F. Ryder, H.Welfare) (1992) *The Buildings of England: Northumberland.* 2nd edition; London

Piggott, S. (1985) *William Stukeley, An Eighteenth Century Antiquary.* 2nd edition; London

*PSAN*, 1, (1855-1857) 45-49 (Society visit to Housesteads – tours Clayton's excavation in SW angle)

*PSAN*, 8 (1898) 213-216 (Society excursion to Bosanquet's excavations)

*PSAN*, 4, (1909-1910) 95-96 (Visit to F.G. Simpson's Kiln, NE & NW angle excavations); 152-153 (Report on exc.)

Ramm, H.G., McDowall, R. W., and Mercer E. (1970) *Shielings and Bastles*. Royal Commission on Historical Monuments (England), London

Richmond, I.A. and Childe, F.A. (1942) 'Gateways of Forts on Hadrian's Wall', *AA*, 20, 134ff

Richmond, I.A. and Simpson, F.G. (1946) (Note on excavation of Turret 36B and broad Wall foundation, in 'Roman Britain in 1945') *JRS*, 36, 134 & 136 fig. 9

Rivet, A.L.F. and Smith, C. (1981) *The Place-names of Roman Britain*. 2nd edition; London.

Roach Smith, C. (1852) *Collectanea Antiqua*. London

Rushworth, A. (ed.) (forthcoming) *The Grandest Station: Excavation and Survey at Housesteads Roman Fort by C.M.Daniels, J.P. Gillam, J.G. Crow, D.J. Smith and the RCHME 1954-88*. English Heritage Archaeological Report, London

Ryder P.F. (1990) *Bastles and Towers in the Northumberland National Park*. (11-12)

Salway, P. (1965) *The Frontier People of Roman Britain*. Cambridge

Simpson, F.G. (1931) (Note on excavation in North gateway, in 'Roman Britain in 1930') *JRS*, 21, 218

Simpson, G. (ed.) (1976) *Watermills and Military Works on Hadrian's Wall*. Kendal

Skinner, J. (ed. H. and P. Coombs) (1978) *Hadrian's Wall in 1801: Observations on the Roman Wall*. (37-39) Bath

Smith, D.J. (1954) *Excavation at Housesteads 1954*. (Typed MS) Department of Archaeology, University of Newcastle upon Tyne

Smith, D.J. (1962) 'The restoration of the "Birth of Mithras" from 'Housesteads', *AA*, 40, 277-280

Smith, D.J. (1968) *Housesteads: South-east angle and a note on the water supply*. (Typed MS). Department of Archaeology, University of Newcastle upon Tyne

Smith, D. J. (forthcoming) 'Excavations in the Principia', in A.Rushworth (ed.) *The Grandest Station: Excavation and Survey at Housesteads Roman Fort by C.M. Daniels, J.P. Gillam, J.G. Crow, D.J. Smith and the RCHME 1954-88*. English Heritage Archaeological Report, London

Smith, I. (1996) 'The origins and development of Christianity in northern Britian and southern Pictland', in J Blair and C Pyrah (ed.) *Church Archaeology, Research directions for the future* CBA Research Report 104, York

Smith, R. (1722) 'Observations upon the Picts Wall', in W. Camden *Britannia* (ed. E. Gibson), II, 1051-1060

Snape, M.E. (1991) 'Roman and Native: vici on the north British frontier', in V.A. Maxfield & M.J. Dobson (eds.) *Roman Frontier Studies 1989*, 468-471, Exeter

Sommers, C.S. (1984) *The Military Vici in Roman Britain. Aspects of their Location, Layout, Administration, Function and End*. BAR 129, Oxford

Stukeley, W. (1759) *The Medallic History of Carausius*. (Vol II), London.

Stukeley, W. (1776) *Iter Boreale of 1725*, in *Itinerarium Curiosum*, 2nd edn., II, London

Swinhow, F. (1752) in *Gentleman's Magazine*, 22, 108

Tait, J. (1963) 'An excavation at Housesteads, 1962', *AA*, 41, 37-44

Taylor, D.J.A. (2000) *The Forts on Hadrian's Wall: A comparative analysis of the form and construction of some buildings*. BAR 305, Oxford

Wallis, J. (1769) *The Natural History and Antiquities of Northumberland*. (Vol. 2), London

Warburton, J. (1716) *A Map of the County of Northumberland*. London

Welfare, H.G. (forthcoming) 'Survey of Housesteads environs', in A. Rushworth (ed.) *The Grandest Station: Excavation and Survey at Housesteads Roman Fort by C.M. Daniels, J.P. Gillam, J.G. Crow, D.J. Smith and the RCHME 1954-88.* English Heritage Archaeological Report, London

Welsby, D.A. (1982) *The Roman Military Defence of the British Provinces in its Later Phases.* BAR 101, Oxford

Welsby, D.A. (1989) Report on the carved stonework at Housesteads. English Heritage

Whitworth, A.M. (1990) 'The Housesteads bastle', *AA*, 18, 127-129

Whitworth, A.M. (1994) 'Recording the Roman Wall', *AA*, 22, 67-77

Whitworth, A.M. (2000) *Hadrian's Wall: Some Aspects of its Post-Roman Influence on the Landscape.* BAR 296, Oxford

Wilkes, J.J. (1960) 'Excavations at Housesteads in 1959'. *AA*, 38, 61-71

Wilkes, J.J. (1961) 'Excavations in Housesteads fort, 1960', *AA*, 39, 279-300

Wilkes, J.J. (1966) 'Early Fourth-Century Rebuilding of Hadrian's Wall', in M.G. Jarret and B. Dobson, *Britain and Rome*, pp 114-138

Woodside, R. and Crow, J.G. (1999) *Hadrian's Wall: An Historic Landscape.* National Trust

# INDEX

*Page references in bold are to illustrations*

If you are interested in purchasing other books published by Tempus, or in case you have difficulty finding any Tempus books in your local bookshop, you can also place orders directly through our website

www.tempus-publishing.com

or from

BOOKPOST, Freepost, PO Box 29, Douglas, Isle of Man IM99 1BQ
Tel 01624 836000   email bookshop@enterprise.net